CHEATING
BUT NOT
CHEATED

A MEMOIR OF THE ATLANTA PUBLIC SCHOOLS CHEATING SCANDAL
2ND EDITION

By: Christopher Waller and
L.B.Jones

Excerpts from Atlanta Journal and Constitution reprinted by permission.

Editing by Joan Guardinella

2nd Edition

www.CheatingbutNotCheated.com

Preface

Christopher Waller

As an educator, the biggest profit I can gain is that a student knows more about a subject after being in my class. For me, this book is not about attempting to make a profit or attempting to redeem myself. This book is about telling the "other side" of a nationwide story. My side is the only way to get a three-dimensional view of the entire cheating scandal. So, I am donating a portion of my profits to my favorite charity, the Haiti Fund of the Sixth Episcopal District of the CME Church in Atlanta, which supports an orphanage for children in Haiti.

LaDawn "LBJ" Blackett Jones

As an attorney and Chris's co-author, my biggest goal is ensuring that I meet my client's goal(s) through my counsel and/or my legal representation. I had hesitations about helping Chris to write his story. However, I could not ignore or deny his earnest need to tell a story about his hard working colleagues and the climate within the school system. Personally, it disturbs me that the issue of over testing is still ignored. As a parent, I hope this book will spark a discussion in the education community.

We joined together to fulfill our individual goals in *Cheating but Not Cheated*, waiving all conflicts of interest and attorney-client privileges for this book. We began our work on this literary document after the representation for the legal case was complete, and we wrote this book with our full informed agreement.

—Christopher Waller and LaDawn B. Jones

Acknowledgments

I would like to thank God for his unwavering grace, which has proved itself sufficient to sustain me. I want to thank my wife, Carolyn. Carolyn, you have been an untiring source of strength and support throughout this entire process. Thank you to my children, who were forced to grow up quickly, dealing with fear of the uncertainty about the future and taunting about this ordeal now and in the years to come. My sons were born during the middle of the controversy and chaos, and they will always bear my name that is forever intertwined with this event. I want to thank the Bishop Kenneth Carter for his guidance and the Butler Street CME Church family for their support throughout this true test of faith. I also must thank my legal team for being direct, honest, consistent, and hardworking. Finally, I want to thank all the other family members and friends who proved themselves to be loyal and faithful. You know who you are.
—Christopher Waller

I want to thank God who made it possible to run a family, a law practice, and a legislative district all while composing this book. I want to thank God for the time that he gave me with my parents while writing this book. I want to thank my husband, Nate Jones, for encouraging me to continue and telling me "I think you have a winner." That was all I needed to go from an idea to a completed story. To my children, Lyndon and Brendon, I hope that watching Mommy dedicate time to achieving goals she sets for herself encourages you to be lifetime achievers. To all those who helped to contribute to the completed book, thank you!
—LaDawn B. Jones

Table of Contents

For information ABOUT THE AUTHORS, please visit:

CheatingbutNotCheated.com

LaDawnJones.com

Introduction

By LaDawn B. Jones

From the moment Christopher Waller walked into my office, he seemed like a character in a book. For more than a year, Chris and I pored through his story, the evidence, and the what-ifs at my desk. I told him trial is not his time to tell what he wanted to say. Much later, he decided to write this book. In the middle of the trial, Chris sent me dozens of audio recordings and said, "I need you to turn this into a book." I listened and talked to Chris about the conflicts of a lawyer writing a book with a client. Chris did not care. He wanted his story told and I understood. He had been the poster child of the Atlanta Public Schools (APS) cheating scandal, and his ego was big enough to handle the scrutiny that would come from his brutal honesty.

Then when I read Rachel Aziz's article in *The New Yorker* while traveling through New York's LaGuardia Airport, I finally agreed with Chris that his story was not being told fairly. The cover illustration and ten-page article focused on the cheating scandal involving Chris as principal of Parks Middle School Although the article included Chris's perspective, it was still told through the point of view of the investigation. There is much more to the story. . . . I text him before my plane took off and told him I would help him write the book he had been asking me to help write. Chris's case had come to a conclusion by his guilty plea and he was no longer my client. I realized for the first time that it wasn't just a local issue. The nation wanted to know how the cheating occurred. And this book, told from Chris's perspective, would highlight what specifically the teachers had done to produce false results.

For a number of reasons, Chris was the best person to tell the scandal's story, which spanned years and included hundreds of educators. He had been exalted as the hero for his success in "beating the odds" as principal of the Parks Middle School. But when a state-led analysis of erasure marks showed that his school had the highest number of tests with human intervention, he was then quickly identified as the villain, becoming the scandal's poster child. Of all the defendants who entered voluntary guilty pleas, his sentence was the toughest. And next to the APS superintendent Dr. Beverly Hall, Chris was the number one face shown during most of the media coverage.

From our first meeting, Chris expressed how his teachers' hard work was never discussed. He swore that they had actually taught the children of Parks Middle School. In addition to telling his side of the story, I also encouraged Chris to use his experience to share what should have been done to improve the scores of the children who lived in the poor community of Southwest Atlanta served by his middle school.

The result is a book that includes all of the above in addition to being a study of educational ethics in light of data, testing, and technology. As the first summary of the scandal from the view of an educator, as opposed to the view of the media or a prosecutor, *Cheating but Not Cheated* may guide policy makers toward practices to detect, prevent, and avoid cheating in schools throughout the United States.

Although Chris insisted on telling his story, he—as he explains in the book—did not always tell the truth, even to his previous lawyers. His breakthrough began the day he decided to come into my office and tell me the real story. His revelations continued throughout the next several, painful meetings during which I had to pry the details out of him. His timing, however, was impeccable.

The month Chris came clean, January 2014, my book club was discussing *Good Self, Bad Self* by Judy Smith. Best known as the real-life fixer who inspired the character of Olivia Pope on the ABC show *Scandal*, Smith describes how she helps her clients solve their personal crises by helping them to know "the very same qualities that can make you a hero can also make you a villain." She explains that most crises start when someone has too much or too little of one or more of these seven traits: ego, denial, fear, ambition, accommodation, patience, and indulgence. According to Smith, "All these attributes can be blessings as well as curses; they're positive qualities when you manage them well and usually create a crisis when you don't."

Smith's words literally jumped off the page at me. I could readily apply what I learned from the book to many of my own clients. However, it was clear none of my clients had the magnitude of ego and denial as Principal Waller. It was that ego that Dr. Hall used to persuade Chris into cheating to advance his career.

Good Self, Bad Self also included an appendix on how to give a sincere apology. Smith says an apology "can be one of the most important elements in preserving your good self and reputation." In that section, she gives some direct advice on strategizing with a crisis client. I followed her steps like a manual: (1) interview the client; (2) find out what he or she wants to say; (3) urge the client to speak from the heart; (4) talk for a long time about what he or she did; (5) find out what the impact was on others; and (6) describe what the client would want to say to those who were hurt.

And the result was a breakthrough by Chris Waller in my office.

Smith required that clients *own* what they did to cause the crisis, not just in the apology but in their minds. Getting Chris to "own" his part was difficult. Even after he could freely say, "I orchestrated the cheating," he couldn't say what he specifically did. When I asked Chris to describe his actions, his vague and passive responses made it appear he was not being forthcoming. As a former prosecutor for the same office as the one handling the case against Chris, I knew what the district attorney would want. If a plea agreement, contingent on telling the truth and testifying at trial, was going to happen, Chris had to be able to say exactly what happened without any uncertainties. But he had been working to disguise what had occurred since 2009, so it was like peeling an onion, layer by layer to get him comfortable with his truth.

While writing this introduction, the trial involving Chris's former colleagues was still in the prosecution phase of what was expected to last at least six months. Chris and I wrote this book during that trial, which meant he would not know the results, including what would happen to those he implicated. Given the timing, *Cheating but Not Cheated* demonstrates Chris's honesty, and his sincere perceptions, opinions, and apologetic stance.

Intertwined within the cheating scandal was the spark that led to the explosion of the culture of cheating, sex, and drugs in the APS system. This case—one of the longest trials in history—became national news, drawing unprecedented news coverage because of its unprecedented criminal prosecution of twelve defendants.

The *Atlanta Journal–Constitution* (*AJC*) credited itself with breaking this story. In fact, the newspaper cited the investigation, which it launched in 2008, throughout its website and coverage of the case. I recalled smiling when I saw a video of a newspaper journalist commenting on his print story on the *AJC* site. The newspaper itself had become one of this case's rock stars. For sure, a Pulitzer and whatever other journalistic awards there are to gain were simply waiting for the conclusion of this trial.

The outcome of the trial is inconsequential. The *AJC*, through its investigation, led to several dozen teachers and administrators admitting on the record that they cheated on the exam. Even if the twelve defendants and Dr. Beverly Hall were found not guilty at trial, the *AJC* had a story. The *AJC* covered no other event, including the 1996 Olympic Games and its bombing, with such fervor.

Having an inside look at District Attorney Paul Howard Jr.'s love/hate relationship with some of the *AJC* journalists and all media was both a blessing and a curse. DA Howard is truly one of the smartest men I know, and I consider him a mentor. However, "the ego" as described in Judy Smith's book fits Howard like a glove. The *AJC* pushed on Howard's known agenda to win big to ensure this was not just a case, but *the* case. Being a visionary beyond his time, Howard is known for hosting a grand ball when a small barbecue would suffice. The *AJC* used that to its advantage.

The published reports of the *AJC* were thorough and are included in this book as a backdrop to what Chris was experiencing and thinking at the time. In addition to a thorough backdrop, the articles also highlight the inseparable and impactful role the media played in this case.

Chapter 1

Cheating but Not Cheated

"September 23, 2014, it is 4:15 a.m., and I have something I need to say . . ."
—Christopher Waller recording for *Cheating but Not Cheated*

I want to clarify the difference between cheating and cheating children. One of the major media frenzies out of this scandal was that children were cheated. After working at the school for more than five years and seeing the means of the students and the families in the Parks Middle School community, I found that charge highly offensive. So, I wanted to take a moment to reflect on why I know children at Parks were not cheated. Cheating did take place at Parks Middle School, but our children were not cheated.

Parks students lived in a very rough community; they also had very low socioeconomic bases. Some of these students were growing up in a single-parent environment; others were living with grandparents; some were raising siblings. We tried to put things in place to make sure the kids came to school every single day, and they recognized the school as a sanctuary. We did not use the "pull the cat out of the hat" approach to academic learning. We taught standards.

1

We taught to the tests. We tutored. We used differentiated instruction. We implemented all the best practices needed to take place for instruction. I'm willing to bet that is what occurred at most, if not all, of the Atlanta Public Schools.

The initial onset of cheating was not to get kids to meet the standard. Cheating started because of the targets that had been handed down from the APS administration. You were constantly in competition against yourself to meet the targets. Even though the kids who performed at one level moved on to another grade level; they set the standard for the grade level behind them. It became increasingly more difficult to meet that target of kids exceeding the standard from year to year. Once you get up beyond the 84th or 85th percentile in a Title I school, it's more difficult to get to the 90th percentile or above.

Schools where at least 35 percent of the children in their attendance area are from low-income families or at least 35 percent of the enrolled students are from low-income families receive federal Title I funding. The proportion of low-income families is most frequently measured by the percentage of students eligible to receive free and reduced-price lunches. Title I funds are to be used for programs designed to improve the academic achievement of children from low-income homes. More than half of all public schools receive funding under Title I throughout the United States.

Because targets continued to grow at a much faster rate than Adequate Yearly Progress (AYP), it became increasingly difficult to meet the target as set by the APS system. AYP is a measurement defined by the No Child Left Behind Act of 2001 that allows the US Department of Education to determine how every public school and school district in the country is performing academically according to results on standardized tests. Superintendent Beverly Hall set the targets for the Atlanta Public Schools to meet each year in testing.

Kids at my school were exposed to a lot of opportunities. Teachers provided both morning and afternoon tutorials. We started contracts with private companies to assist the teachers. Educators would take kids out of class to hold additional tutorial groups during the day to help students catch up, as well as Saturday tutorials. We held lock-ins at the school to prepare kids for the writing test. Several teachers stayed after work and were not paid extra to prepare for these extra teaching sessions. How many people would do that in their professions?

We sent our kids to places that their peers in other schools never had a chance to go. We wanted the kids to realize that the world was much larger than the community in which they resided. Our kids had opportunities to go on trips to Canada, Washington, DC, and the rain forests of Puerto Rico. We organized and ran trips that went above and beyond what was expected of us as educators. Even though the parents could not pay for those trips, we found a way. We raised money. We gave money. We made sure that no child was left out who deserved to go. We wanted our students to be exposed to other areas of the world. All of our children had opportunities to participate in extracurricular activities, whether they could afford it or not. If the parents could not pay for uniforms, supplies, camps, or other needs, we found a way to make it happen. We made certain to include each and every kid in all kinds of activities. If an activity was done at any other school in APS, the kids at Parks had—if not the same activity or better activity—they had a similar activity. They were never left behind.

We made sure that our teachers had the proper professional development. We evaluated teachers and sent them to workshops and we gave workshops to make sure that teachers taught and students learned. Nobody wants to talk about the success of the students at Parks. We didn't follow the kids to high school. So, we couldn't witness for ourselves what Patrick E. did when he went to high school, how he graduated first in his class. We didn't follow Montanez B. to high school. We didn't follow any of the kids over to high school. If we had followed them to high school, we would have seen a lot of them go to college and succeed in college. And some of them who went to college would not have gone to college had they not had the support that we were able to give them while they were students at Parks.

Students increased their self-esteem; they started seeing things differently. They saw a way out. One of the major things that I want to really make sure that we put on the record, and as a part of what we do and say, is that there was cheating, but the children at Parks were not cheated. I would argue that you would not get a child from Parks who would really tell you directly that they missed out on something academically or socially because of the erasures that took place at school.

I am not suppressing or denying the fact that cheating took place at Parks. I am simply stating that even though there was cheating, the children were not cheated. The children were held in the highest regard and in the heart of everybody in that school. As a matter of fact, you didn't come to work there if you didn't. If you didn't have a passion for those kids, you couldn't work at Parks Middle School.

Working at Parks required passion. It was not a nine-to-five job. You had to adopt children, sponsor clubs, send kids on trips, buy clothes, and more. It was not a typical go-to-work-at-nine-get-off-at-five type of school. You had to have a passion to work in that neighborhood. I cannot think of anyone who took a job under my leadership at Parks Middle School that didn't have a passion for the kids in the Southwest Atlanta community and the work that it took in order to make the children successful.

There are many students from Parks who have finished high school, finished college, some in graduate school, law school, or medical school. They're making a difference in our local, national, and global communities. Children were not cheated, even though cheating did take place. The *AJC* did not report these things.

Surge in CRCT results raises 'big red flag'[i]

Updated: 1:36 p.m. Monday, March 26, 2012 | Posted: 1:29 p.m. Sunday, Dec. 14, 2008

By John Perry and Heather Vogell

An AJC analysis in December 2008 first reported statistically improbable increases in scores on the Criterion-Referenced Competency Test at an Atlanta school. This is the original article.

A miracle occurred at Atherton Elementary this summer, if its standardized math test scores are to be believed.

Half of the DeKalb County school's fifth graders failed a yearly state test in the spring.

When the 32 students took retests, not only did every one of them pass — 26 scored at the highest level.

The AJC's original APS Cheating Scandal reports

No other Georgia fifth grade pulled off such a feat in the past three years. It was, as one researcher put it, as extraordinary as a snowstorm in July. In Atlanta.

Atherton Principal James Berry said the scores were the product of intense tutoring.

But state education officials said last week they will investigate steep gains at Atherton and four other schools as a result of The

Atlanta Journal-Constitution's inquiries.

"It's a big red flag," said Kathleen Mathers, executive director of the Governor's Office of Student Achievement. She said officials don't know what caused the Criterion-Referenced Competency Test scores to soar, only that they require explanation.

The state has not routinely mined test data for such anomalies. But officials said it will begin to do so soon, employing widely accepted statistical methods similar to what the AJC used.

Expert: Atherton's improvement 'miraculous'

Atherton's unlikely performance was one of a handful the AJC uncovered by analyzing student scores on the CRCT and retest. The surges were so far outside the norm they raise questions about whether those schools' retest scores are valid.

As a result, the findings also suggest some schools — such as Atherton — that relied on the retest to reach academic goals might not have met federal standards.

Atherton originally placed in the 10th percentile among Georgia fifth grades on the math test, meaning 90 percent of the 1,200 plus schools scored better, the newspaper's study shows.

After the retest, Atherton jumped to the 77th percentile. The move was unduplicated by any school statewide.

The Atherton student with what was likely the biggest gain answered just 16 math questions correctly his first time taking the test — a slightly better result than a student could expect after guessing on all 60 multiple-choice questions.

On the retest, however, the unidentified boy joined the ranks of high scorers, answering 50 questions correctly. Students needed 29 right to pass.

Two experts said the school's rocket ride to the top tier may be too good to be true. They said educators have yet to discover methods that would cause such a jump.

"We don't know of any interventions that do this," said Gregory Cizek, a testing expert at the University of North Carolina.

Improving so many scores so much after 18 days of summer school, he said, "is miraculous." He likened it to a July blizzard.

In an interview, principal Berry said the school made a tremendous summer-school effort to address failing students' weaknesses. "This was all but giving blood," he said. "I pulled out every stop known to man."

Asked whether he had any concerns about test security or score validity, Berry said: "Oh my God, I hope not. I know the people that I chose were pretty honest. I would hope that that wasn't the case. Well, I can honestly say to you that I don't think that that was the case at all."

DeKalb school official suspects scoring error

DeKalb school officials are investigating because of the AJC's questions, spokesman Dale Davis said.

Tom Bowen, vice chairman of DeKalb's school board, said it was hard to believe that retest prep would make so much of a difference for so many students.

He suspects a score-processing error, he said, but impropriety remains a possibility. He said he welcomed the investigations.

"The children who receive these scores are not served if these scores aren't valid," Bowen said. "They would get a false sense of their achievement level."

Atherton's spectacular fifth-grade retest scores bumped the school into compliance with the federal "adequate yearly progress" standard under the No Child Left Behind Act.

This year was the first that federal authorities let Georgia districts and schools use retest scores in that calculation. It meant the retests, traditionally used to decide whether to retain children, took on new significance as a last resort for schools desperate to make the grade and avoid penalties.

In addition to undergoing closer state monitoring, schools that don't meet federal standards lose prestige and run the risk of losing students — and the state money that comes with them — to other schools.

In the metro area, two other schools also made extraordinary gains. Like Atherton, each met federal standards only because of retest gains.

Adamsville in Atlanta had 48 percent improvement rate

In Atlanta, 19 of 19 fifth graders at

Adamsville Elementary took and passed the CRCT math retest, state data show. Statewide, only about half of retesters passed at each school. Adamsville students' scores increased an average of 48 points, compared to the state average of 16 points.

Principal Sharon Suitt said her school, like others, identified what tasks students did poorly during the spring test and focused on them in summer school.

"It was an all-concerted effort to make sure they were successful," she said.

Suitt conceded Adamsville's strategy was similar to that of other schools. She said her school tried to boost student self-esteem and was "just really working to motivate students, encouraging them and letting them know they could do it."

She said she did not have concerns about whether the exams were secure or the scores valid.

The Atlanta district has no plans to investigate, spokesman Joe Manguno said in an e-mail. The school developed a learning plan for each student, he said. Classes were taught by teachers who had demonstrated success with the spring CRCT.

"We are satisfied that the gains were valid and defensible," Manguno wrote.

Fulton's Parklane school shot ahead

At Fulton County's Parklane Elementary, 22 of 24 fifth-graders who failed the math CRCT passed the retest. The school outperformed three others in Fulton that shared summer school classes at Parklane.

Principal Lee Adams said Parklane also zeroed in on
students' weaknesses. He said the summer program used a
traditional teaching approach centered on basic skills.
Students are more serious during the summer, he added.

Adams said he didn't know what his school did differently from other schools
to produce such large gains. But he said he, too, was not worried about test
tampering.

"We're the closest school to the district office.

We make sure we're always on our P's and Q's because you never know when
someone is going to come out."

Fulton officials do not see a need to investigate the gains, spokeswoman Susan
Hale wrote in an e-mail. Parklane students received targeted instruction and a
visit from Superintendent Cindy Loe at the beginning of the summer to
encourage them.

"The summer school scores are the result of the hard work of both the teachers
and students at Parklane," she said.

Two other schools, one each in Glynn County and Gainesville, also stuck out
in the newspaper's analysis of test and retest scores. A spokesman for the
Glynn district said its gains were the result of thorough remediation. A
Gainesville official declined to comment.

The AJC's study used a common statistical measurement called standard
deviation to measure how much schools' score increases differed from the average
gain.

At the five schools in question, gains were more than four standard deviations above the average, the analysis showed. That meant the schools outpaced others to an unusually high degree.

"It's concerning, and certainly it signals to you you need to look more closely to see what's going on," said Mathers, of the state achievement office.

Atherton's scores were nine standard deviations above the average. "You don't have 30 kids change on an average of nine standard deviations," Cizek said after reviewing the newspaper's analysis.

Experts said improprieties that could cause such gains include test tampering by an adult, student cribbing or coaching by exam monitors. Or, some teachers may have taught much more closely to the test than others — a practice some consider cheating.

State education officials will look more closely at the five schools the newspaper identified with the biggest average gains, said Stephen Pruitt, state associate superintendent for assessment and accountability. Others that were less dramatic standouts also may be examined, he said.

An investigation could include more data analysis and conversations with school officials. It also could involve what's called an erasure analysis, which looks for an abnormal number or pattern of changed answers on students' bubbled test sheets.

A group of state education officials will discuss the five schools at a meeting after the holidays, Pruitt said. They will begin collecting information from the schools right away and will consider each individually, he said.

The group could refer cases to the Professional Standards Commission, which polices educator credentials, or the student achievement office, which can perform a school audit. Such an audit could involve interviews with students and teachers.

Unfavorable findings could lead the state Board of Education to revoke a school's status as meeting federal standards.

The two state education agencies have begun toughening oversight of the school-reported data used to calculate adequate yearly progress.

"We've got a governor and a superintendent that are very serious about the integrity of our data," Mathers said of Gov. Sonny Perdue and Superintendent Kathy Cox.

State officials emphasized they believe the vast majority of Georgia educators are trying to play by the rules.

Some experts say high-stakes testing has fueled the motivation to cheat on standardized tests.

Tom Haladyna, a professor emeritus at Arizona State University and a testing expert who also examined the AJC's data, noted nine schools had changes three standard deviations or higher.

"These are astounding results," he said.

Haladyna said states should investigate unusual gains more regularly to weed out corrupted scores. In general, he and Cizek said, most teachers are honest. They have suffered over the years because of those who aren't.

"Your school is published as a nonattaining school while these others that have maybe taken liberties are celebrated as high achieving," Haladyna said. "It shames all of us in education to have this happen."

Chapter 2

Plea Deal

My experience with taking a plea occurred in two phases. The first phase was my discussions with my attorneys and the plea negotiations with the assistant district attorneys. The second distinct phase was actually entering a plea of *guilty* to criminal charges at the courthouse.

It took a lot to bring me around to realize that my script did not completely make sense in light of the evidence against me. Again, I need to say for the record, most of my script was true. The only thing that was left out of my original script to my lawyers, family, and colleagues was the fact that I was aware of cheating at Parks Middle School. I didn't immediately fess up that I was aware of cheating at a lot of schools. I was aware of a whole lot of stuff in the district. The Atlanta Public Schools had a very interesting culture; it was one of cheating, drugs, alcohol, and sex. It had a lot of different things going on within that culture.

I had hired a diverse legal team and spent a lot of time with them before I entered my plea. My number one question was: "Will we win?" Although my legal team was confident we could win, once we got to a point of seriously preparing for trial, my attorneys were also sure that politics was playing a large role. Every part of the case was new and unexplored territory. From my point of view and with input from my legal team, the bonds were unprecedented especially in light of our profession; the organized crime indictment without drugs

15

or violence; and the loss of the Garrity motion to suppress employee statements made me feel this case was not being treated like a normal case. This made the answer to the question for my legal team much more difficult to address. We began to really walk through the same questions again: What happened? How did it happen? When did it happen and who did it happen to?

First, I hired the well-known firm of Garland, Samuel & Loeb. One of my good friends, who since passed away, had recommended them, and I made a commitment to him that I would use them if the indictment ever came. He did tell me they would be very expensive, but they would be the best firm to represent me. John Garland and Don Samuel had been practicing criminal defense work for more than thirty years in their firm based out of the Buckhead community in Atlanta. Their list of clients included professional athletes, Hollywood celebrities, and kingpins. I trusted their legal knowledge, their understanding of the district attorney, and their courtroom skills. They had literally "written the book" on criminal law in Georgia.

Then another incident pointed me toward Don. While I was still principal at Parks, my goddaughter was killed in a terrible accident, riding in a car that belonged to me on Easter Sunday, April 12, 2009. In a chain reaction, five people in two separate cars, including my goddaughter and her parents, were killed. The case made the news statewide because the driver of a third vehicle, who had caused the accident, fled the scene. There was a massive search and pleading for this driver to come forward. It was later determined that Aimee Michael, a twenty-three-year-old, had caused the accident and attempted to cover up the damage to her vehicle with the help of her mother. ADA Tanya Miller tried that case, and Michael was sentenced to fifty years in prison. After the trial, I went to eat with some of the prosecutors in the case. I will never forget when one of the district attorneys on the case said that Don Samuel would be the person she would hire if she ever needed criminal defense. That referral from an ADA and my promise to my friend sealed the deal for me working with Don. He was my first call when rumors of the APS scandal broke.

Before Garland, Samuel & Loeb, I had been working with Warren Fortson, who was not a criminal attorney, but an education attorney. He still assisted with the case but did not stay on the team.

I later hired a solo practitioner, LaDawn Blackett Jones, and her firm, The LBJ Law Group, LLC, several months later. She had been recommended highly by one of my good friends who now pastors the church that LaDawn attended when they were both children. My friend said LaDawn was ethical and a hard worker. Unlike my other counsel, LaDawn's practice was brand-new. In fact, she was still in diapers when Don and John had started their practices. LaDawn had recently left the Fulton County District Attorney's office where my case was being prosecuted. She had opened her own practice so that she could run for the office of State Representative. She won her seat and worked on my case during the legislative session. Coincidentally, her representative's office was just steps away from the governor's office where the decision to conduct an erasure analysis had been made.

I also chose LaDawn because I wanted a female lawyer on my legal team, someone who understood how to work in the anomaly that is the Fulton County courts. Although Don has successfully represented dozens of African Americans, I knew race had a lot to do with my case. And having LaDawn, a black woman, on my team also made me a little more comfortable. Many have remarked that had this case occurred anywhere other than a majority African American city and a majority African American school district, the outcome would have been starkly different. There was cheating reported in other school districts around the country and in other parts of Georgia. Yet the only one garnering this type of attention and scrutiny was the mostly African American school system.

Plus, LaDawn knew the Fulton County District Attorney's office. She had just left there as the chief senior ADA a few years before. Early on, she told me that she wouldn't promise any favors as a result of her former position, but she did feel her relationships would help her evaluate what the prosecutors said and their intentions. She would know if they were being genuine and what the DA's office would need to arrive at a mutually acceptable solution. Moreover, she was a stickler for details.

I wanted to make sure I had all of my bases covered. I put together the best diverse team that my money could buy, and I was very confident and comfortable with each of the attorneys on the team. Each one helped me navigate and accept the fact that admitting the truth would not be the end of the world. My attorneys let me know they needed the truth to better prepare themselves to represent me.

Although having a great team was well worth the expense, it also gave an impression that I was financially well-off. During the investigation, I had remarked that I did not have to cheat to gain bonus checks because a principal's salary was pretty good. In addition, I received a salary for being a minister and had business investments that yielded income. My legal team told me what the DA's office had concluded from my statements and my high-end defense team. Somehow that all translated to the Fulton County DA's office that I was rich. The requirement to pay $50,000 as restitution as part of the plea agreement showed their impression of my personal wealth. To date, no other defendant had to pay such high amounts.

Prior to the indictment, Don and LaDawn had spoken with District Attorney Howard in his office. They wanted to know what I could do to avoid indictment altogether. The DA's response was noncommittal. He wanted me to do and say things that I could not do and say, and he wanted the one fish that was bigger than me: Dr. Hall, superintendent of the Atlanta Public Schools. Howard wanted me to go in and say that Dr. Hall had told me to cheat. The prosecutors wanted to know all the details: the place, the specifics, how the cheating was orchestrated among the several schools. Howard wanted me to paint a neat and clean picture of cheating as he wanted to believe it occurred. But this is not what happened. And even with that request, he wanted jail time—in the realm of a year in jail with probation on the end if I made his case. It was a very short meeting.

At the time of that initial meeting, Tanya Miller became the second lead ADA on the case. Eleanor Ross had been the previous ADA on the case, but she had been appointed to a state court judge's position in the neighboring "black" county by the governor, the same governor who led the initial investigation into the cheating scandal. During the APS trial, President Obama selected Ross to fill a federal judge seat in Georgia. ADA Miller was an experienced attorney and made it clear during and after that meeting that she believed I deserved jail time. My attorneys reported to me that during the meeting, DA Howard had turned to ADA Miller and said, "If it was up to just ADA Miller, the offer would include more than one or two years of jail time." After Miller left the DA's office, ADA Fani Willis took over the case. Eventually, the case was indicted, and the real court process began.

The judge had made it very clear in court that if we didn't do a plea deal and we lost the case, I would be spending some serious time in jail as the poster child of the cheating in the media. And the judge insisted that anybody in their right mind, who realized that their stuff wasn't perfect, would try to work through some kind of negotiations with the district attorney.

LaDawn and ADA Willis met privately. The two were friends outside of court and were able to have a very real and very frank conversation about a plea deal. ADA Willis gave LaDawn the case against me as she saw it. LaDawn made the argument that they needed me to get the person they really wanted, Dr. Hall. LaDawn also laid the groundwork for what was my reality. I was a pawn in this system of cheating. Fani's offer, plead to one charge. They basically said, "Pick one." It could have been anything. Pick a charge and plead to it. It didn't make a difference which charge. To make the plea deal work, I only had one obligation: I would have to tell the truth, period. I couldn't deviate from the whole truth. Tell the truth about anything and tell the truth about everything.

At this point, almost four years had gone by since the allegations of cheating surfaced. So, by now, everyone had had their opportunity to go and do whatever they needed to do. Some confessed at first blush. Some had lawyered up and then confessed. We didn't know who had confessed, how the witnesses' stories had changed or grown. By now, people were getting distant and disappearing. Others were looking friendly when they saw me in public, and I couldn't tell if they were throwing me under the bus or kept up their original stories. By the time I went down to the DA's office, I didn't know who had told them what and who had said what. I didn't have the liberty of knowing what truth was the truth on the table. All I could really focus on was telling the truth as I knew it.

I remember opening up my plea status by telling them, "I don't have anything real good to tell you today. All that I'm going to tell you is bad and I'm responsible for it." As I began to talk and say the things I had in my mind for weeks, the ADA said, "Wait a minute. We don't want to talk about what you've done. We know what you've done. Everybody else has told us what you've done." I started to say, *But I haven't told you what I've done in my defense.* Then I felt someone kick me under the table. It was my attorney. I closed my mouth. A kick was my cue. LaDawn had prepped me to shut up if I got kicked. And that kick was hard: it meant to shut up real quick. So, I did, and the ADA repeated, "We don't want to know what you did. We already know what you did. We want to talk about what Dr. Hall did."

I wasn't surprised. In preparing me for the meeting, my attorney told me that was what they wanted to know. From LaDawn's talk with ADA Willis, it was clear the DA's office needed more to get Dr. Hall. LaDawn and I had painstakingly gone through the direct connections of my actions with Dr. Hall's knowledge and involvement. LaDawn had numbered the things we came up with and broke them down in a little color-coded chart, so we had something to refer to when we spoke to the DA's office. LaDawn knew that I could easily go down a rabbit hole and start talking about all the good we did for the kids. She also knew, from our many preparatory meetings, that I could begin speculating on things to which I had no direct knowledge of. To keep me focused on what the DA's office wanted, she pulled out of me seven direct actions of Dr. Hall and her administration that showed cheating occurred under their direction.

In the DA's office, we began to talk about Dr. Hall's interactions with principals, which was minimal. We discussed her leadership style as well as my perception of her. When I tell you "at length," we talked at length. We discussed things without even touching on my specific actions for hours. In the next process, we would talk about Michael Pitts, the executive director of the School Reform Team (SRT) 2, and his work with us, with principals, and specifically his work with Parks and with me. We did it at length again, with very little discussion about what I had personally done. At the very end, I think they may have spent about an hour and a half talking about me, what I thought about me, what I thought I had done, and my part in the whole scandal. They weren't interested so much in what I had to say about my part. They were only interested in what I had to say about Dr. Hall and Pitts. Just like LaDawn, ADA Willis pulled out a piece of paper and said, "Give me ten things that Hall and Pitts did to coordinate and lead cheating in APS that you have direct knowledge of." Ten items were hard. LaDawn and I struggled to get to seven solid indicators. Several things LaDawn had thrown out as not credible enough were brought up. LaDawn didn't want me to seem as though I was making connections that were not there just to get the attention off of me. But the DA's office was interested in all of it. They were convinced by the end that although I was responsible for my part in this, I was chosen because I was a naive young principal who would do whatever it took to succeed.

My plea took several hours, and it happened over several days. Ironically, I was indicted on Good Friday, and the first day I sat down with the DA's office for my plea was a Sunday. I had to report there at 10:00 a.m. on Sunday.

The prosecutors knew that I was a minister. Yet, they wanted me to come down on a Sunday at 10:00 a.m. And when I arrived, the first thing the ADA said to me was: "We didn't think you'd be able to come because you're a minister." I felt like this was a test to see if I was really committed. Another part of me thought it was a setup for failure. LaDawn told me it was to beat the judge's plea deadline scheduled for that week. Anyone who did not enter a plea by his deadline was going to trial. This deadline had been extended two previous times, but to everyone's knowledge this was it. My attorneys tried to convince me that since I was entering a plea, I was no longer a defendant. Now, I was a witness, and as a witness, the State of Georgia was on my side and would help me through this process. I was not at all convinced. I was concerned every question was a trick or a setup to ensure they could still send me to trial and convict me. After a multiple-count RICO indictment and multimillion-dollar bond, I was certain that the DA's office was out for my blood.

We were there Sunday at 10:00 a.m. until Sunday night at 10:00 p.m. We were back Monday, all day, and it seems like we were back again on Tuesday. We were there three or four days, all day, long hours, working through the plea. The DA's office provided pizza and salads for the staff, me, and my legal team. We sat at the tiny conference table in that small room for hours. It was not in the traditional district attorney's office in the county courthouse. This office space assigned to the APS cheating case team was across the street in the much nicer and newer government building. As you walk down the hallway, you saw how it was a badge of honor to be assigned to this case. The staff had pictures of the team, the APS team sign, and other decor not common in a prosecutor's office. The team had been working together for several years. Most attorneys and staff at this office had several dozen, if not hundreds of cases per attorney and assistant. The attorneys assigned to this case, however, had one job and one job only. You could tell by their demeanor, their attention to time and details that they were focused. I learned from LaDawn that leading up to the trial and all throughout, the attorneys were working six, sometimes seven days every week on this case. The evidence in this case made up more than a terabyte of info. A terabyte of electronic info is like putting the Library of Congress on a hard drive.

To say they were dedicated to this case was an understatement. When interviewing me, the DA's office was making sure that the details were in place and that there was not a lot of miscommunication or play on words. All the work that had gone into this case was not going to be ruined by the likes of me. What was signed off on is what had been said and what had been agreed would be testified upon. Period. At some point, we completed the plea. But throughout the process, I had lots of time to ponder the people who held my fate in their hands.

The DA's office had assigned a true cast who would play out very well in a made-for-television movie. I knew ADA Clint Rucker a little bit from his work with the case with my goddaughter. Rucker came across as a cool, clean-cut, fair guy. He didn't appear to be slimy or sneaky. He carried the appearance of a kind-of fair person, just a human being doing his job. It helped me a little bit with him being in the room. LaDawn says it is because our egos spoke to each other silently. We were both large men with very large personalities. Rucker had a connection with people, particularly jurors. They trusted him and the way he spoke. I could now see why. He was the anti-prosecutor. Being questioned by him wasn't like a cross-examination. My wife seemed tougher than he did. But he still got you to speak to him. You felt like it was just the two of you in a room when he began to talk to you. Even if I had considered going in and not telling the whole truth, Rucker would have made me tell the truth.

ADA Willis was the newest assigned lead prosecutor on the case. It didn't take but a minute to get to know her style. She's very transparent, a glass-house kind of person. What you see is what you get. It is what it is. She will tell you what she was thinking and what she wanted. So, she was an easy person to learn, more organized, no nonsense, straight to the point, almost like New Jersey–style person. During my plea, she wasn't very harsh but was direct and right to the point. Blunt, this is what it is, this is what it ain't. I was concerned that Willis didn't like me personally. Initially, from what I had learned from my attorneys about her conversations about me, I had the impression that she thought I was scum. But in person, I could see she had turned a corner on me. In fact, I believe she went to bat for me to have my sentence reduced from the original offer from DA Howard. I never confirmed this, but for some reason I believe she convinced him that my role was not what they originally thought.

I also remember ADA April McConnell really helping me at the initial part of the plea. In the beginning, I remained a little apprehensive and defensive despite the fact I was cooperating. ADA McConnell was very soft-spoken, very sweet, very gentle, and non-abrasive. She had a gift of disarming you. When I made a statement to respond to a question and I was very matter-of-fact, she would say in a very grandma-like tone, "But could it have been . . ." or "Do you think it could have been . . ." or "Look at it from the other side," and "Can you see how . . ." Each time, I was totally disarmed. She chipped away my initial fears. Because of her disarming approach, she made me reconsider facts that I had gone over again and again in my head. They made connections for me that I had not made on my own. For example, I knew Dr. Hall had chosen me to go on special trips and conferences around the country. But through her questioning, ADA McConnell made me realize Dr. Hall was putting together "her team." She was rewarding those who had been loyal. She was helping to keep her team happy and kept them lockstep by taking them (us) on special trips. Not until I sat in the room in the DA's office and listed all the people who had gone on these conferences did I realize that Dr. Hall had organized her team of cheaters. Although we never discussed cheating on these trips, we did build a bond with one another that would allow this ruse to continue as long as it did.

After my plea, the next time I would see ADA McConnell was on television. Shortly before the APS trial was scheduled to begin, her estranged husband shot her and a passenger in her vehicle in the head. He then went to a cemetery and took his own life. ADA McConnell survived. But as the news reported on the shooting, I went to pray for her. My church was very close to the hospital where she was first treated. My intention, of course, was to go pray for her and her recovery. I didn't know her prior to this case. But I could tell from the way the prosecutors handled the case, I was not their enemy. They were doing their jobs. They never treated me disrespectfully or harshly. I had no hard feelings or ill-will for them. I did wish they dropped the case against me completely, but I knew that was not an option and under the circumstances, I had gotten a good deal. Of course, as I left the chapel of the hospital, the news media immediately jumped on me, wondering why I was there.

Once the info hit the news I had visited the hospital and appeared on the news, my legal team went crazy. At that time, ADA McConnell's husband had not been found and everyone was a suspect. It may have not been the smartest thing to visit and appear on the media when I could have easily been made suspect number one. However, my sincere respect for how ADA McConnell treated me was all I had on my mind at the time.

During the plea preparation, I was questioned by each of the ADAs together and separately. Every question that was asked, I answered truthfully. I didn't try to protect anybody. I didn't try to hide anything. I didn't try to cover up anything. I gave straightforward responses. I took responsibility for my part in the APS cheating scandal more directly as it related to Parks Middle School. That responsibility was reduced to a ten-plus-page document that outlined in detail every single thing I admitted to doing while at Parks. It took several drafts to get it correct.

Shortly after we completed the plea agreement, we had to go to court to enter my plea on the record. My attorneys were very clear about what I should wear and what my demeanor should be in the courtroom. They wanted to be certain nothing would derail our plea agreement. I didn't have the opportunity to be arrogant. I didn't have the opportunity to make it about vindicating myself or telling the full story I am telling you now. I had to practice humility. At this point, in order to get a deal that would keep me out of jail, I had to throw myself on the mercy of the court.

A part of my plea included an apology letter. My attorneys told me they would help me with the wording. During the plea process, they just wrote it for me. "Don't worry about it, I'll just write it for you," Don told me during the plea process. Much like LaDawn knew what the DA's office wanted to hear during the plea deal, Don knew what the judge and public wanted to hear. I had an opportunity to look at it while in the DA's office, but I was in the middle of a marathon debriefing, and my mind was focused on that and the questions whirling around my head: How I was doing? Did they believe me? How long before this is over? I approved the letter without really even looking at it. Afterward, when my mind was clearer, I asked Don to let me see it. He never would let me see it. He put it in my hand one minute before it was time for me to read it. I had never really read it before. I had never seen it before, but together my attorneys captured my innermost thoughts and sincere apology.

That day, I walked into the wood-paneled walls of the courtroom. I had on a suit, no tie, as suggested by my attorneys. No expensive jewelry. I was not to smile or laugh. Plain face. The media was there, and their cameras were focused squarely on me the entire time. As the proceedings started, ADA Willis began reading the multi-paged plea agreement. At one point, there was a typo that made it sound like I had inappropriate sexual contact with students. I looked at my team and shook my head so hard it caught the judge's attention. To my legal team, the reading of the plea agreement was just a formality that did not change the outcome of what would happen that day. For me, however, this was my life on paper. To me, this was a discussion that would follow me forever. It was very difficult for me to admit to my actions initially, so I certainly was not prepared to take responsibility for things I did not do. Particularly things that was harmful to the children in the school. As I said before, what we did was not to hurt the children. We taught our children, and I did not want that point to be overrun by any incorrect statements. Not to mention, the media had made this story their shot at a Pulitzer or other

Christopher Waller's Sentencing Document

reporting rewards. A plea that included sexual abuse against children that stemmed from allegations for cheating is exactly the type of thing they would have played on repeat for weeks. The error was corrected on the record, and ADA Willis acknowledged it was an error. Then the plea continued.

After entering a guilty plea to one count of false statements and writings, a felony, I was sentenced to five years on probation. The special conditions of my probation required me to do a thousand hours of community service and pay $50,000 in restitution to APS and to cover fees and court cost for the time expended on this case. The plea agreement included having the probation suspended after I finished my restitution and community service. I also was able to take the plea as a first offender. This meant that after everything was complete, my criminal record would be cleared, and I could honestly say I was not a convicted felon. The arrest would also be expunged from my record. My sentence was longer than the previous people who pled and my fines by far were the worst. Both my legal counsel and I have several theories on why that occurred.

I then had to approach the podium with my attorney to do my part and apologize. Until now, I had not spoken out loud. I had been seated the entire time. Now all six feet four inches of me had to go forward to wrap up this entire four-year process. When I read my apology for the first time, I was reading it to the judge. Emotions I never imagined arose in me. The apology letter took all that I had said and done and put it in black and white. It made me realize firsthand how awful I had been. Although I thought I was helping, I could see how it could have easily been perceived that I was not helping the school system. I could see that it could be perceived that what I was doing was only hurting. Worst of all, it appeared that I was hurting others for my own good. Those others were not just the children; it was my staff and teachers who had dedicated themselves to Parks.

That took a toll on me, because I had spent my life trying to help others, trying to serve others, trying to solve others' problems, and trying to fix other folks' stuff. But in reading that letter, I realized that I had been engaged in criminal activity. Educators don't go to school to get involved with racketeering. I promise you: we don't go to school to do anything criminal.

I believe had any educator known—although I can only speak for myself—that participating in any way with changing answers on tests would have been judged a criminal matter, they would not have done it. Did we know we were taking a risk of being terminated? Sure. Did we consider our teaching certificates could be suspended? Yes. But a crime for which you could be prosecuted for up to twenty years in prison? Never. But it occurred and here is my story about how that happens.

APOLOGY LETTER

To: Judge Baxter
Letter of Apology

The students and parents of Parks Middle School,

I am standing here to plead guilty to my participation in the cheating activity at Parks Middle School. I orchestrated cheating by several teachers and fostered a culture of cheating that continued even after I was not at the school. As the factual statement read by the prosecutor shows, my role was continuous for several years and I accept responsibility for this conduct which was unethical, immoral, dishonest and criminal.

This conduct harmed the students. It harmed the reputation of the school; it harmed the reputation of the entire school system and the City of Atlanta.

For many years, I have tried to rationalize what I did. I am through rationalizing and making excuses and I am no longer interested in blaming others. There were others who participated in this conduct with me. But they are not responsible for my criminal acts.

I want to say something about the teachers in my school, some of whom have been the subject of this criminal case, others of whom were not prosecuted.

These were extremely dedicated teachers. I want you to know that these were hardworking, dedicated teachers who were devoted to the children and to teaching them.

This does not change the fact that they cheated (not all teachers, but many)—and that they did so at my direction and as orchestrated by me. But the cheating does not in any way change the fact that these teachers worked hard. They cared about the children. And they were great teachers.

No matter how hard the teachers worked, however, and no matter how much we actually improved the school, there was no way that we could keep up with targets. The targets were unattainable. At least not by legitimate means. So we cheated to attain the targets. And then many of us—not the least of which was me—tried to cover up this conduct. I made false statements to the investigators. I lied about my participation.

I don't know what long-term effect this conduct will have on the teachers, the school, and the City, but I hope that this criminal case and the fact that so many of are finally accepting responsibility, will have some positive effect on the school and the community. Hopefully, my community service will also, to some extent, make some improvement in the students' lives.

I want to thank the prosecutors who have been generous in their recommendation. I know that Mr. Howard and Ms. Willis and Mr. Rucker have had to endure considerable criticism for bringing this case. I hope the students, and the community—and the teachers who did what I encouraged them to do—will accept this apology.

Christopher Waller

Chapter 3

Under Investigation

From AJC.com

Defense challenges meeting between Beverly Hall, investigator

Posted 7:48 p.m. Monday, October 6, 2014
By Molly Bloom The Atlanta Journal-Constitution

A private investigator testified Monday he was stunned when Atlanta Public Schools Superintendent Beverly Hall and other top APS officials did not seem overly concerned about his conclusion that test-cheating occurred at Parks Middle School.

"I just couldn't believe it," Reginal Dukes testified during the APS test-cheating trial. "I thought it was pretty serious. . . . I just anticipated more from them."

Dukes said he reported his findings on May 10, 2006, during a meeting with Hall and other top APS officials, including then-regional superintendent Michael Pitts, one of 12 defendants on trial.

But Pitts' defense attorney, George Lawson, questioned whether the meeting occurred at all.

"I understand you are contending you met with Dr. Hall," Lawson told Dukes, repeatedly making that point to jurors. During Lawson's questioning, it became clear that he will argue to jurors that the meeting never happened.

Lawson did all he could to contradict Dukes' recitation of what happened, even noting discrepancies of his account with APS visitors' sign-in sheets. Meanwhile, Fulton County prosecutor Clint Rucker tried to bolster Dukes' testimony by calling on a caterer who delivered lunch to Hall's conference room that day.

Dukes' testimony is particularly important in the case against Pitts. Prosecutors are trying to show that Pitts, who oversaw Parks Middle School, was told about test-cheating there and did nothing about it.

Dukes could also be an eventual prosecution witness against Hall, who is not on trial at this time because she is recovering from treatment for Stage IV breast cancer.

Even though Dukes said he found test cheating at Parks, the school's principal, Christopher Waller, was never disciplined. Waller has pleaded guilty and acknowledged he continued to pressure his teachers to cheat on state-mandated standardized tests.

Dukes, a former Atlanta cop, said he was hired by APS in 2006 as an external investigator to look into allegations of test cheating at Parks Middle, as well as other misconduct by Waller.

During his investigation, Dukes said, he learned that a "prompt" had been given to students weeks before they were administered the writing test. The students, he testified, were given several questions but told to focus on Question No. 7: Identify a rule you think is unfair in your home, school or community and describe why you think it's unfair and explain why you would change it.

On the actual writing test the word "rule" was replaced by "law," he said.

This was strong evidence that cheating had occurred, said Dukes, noting he interviewed more than a dozen students who corroborated the misconduct. On May 10, 2006, Dukes said, he was called to the APS central office to present his findings to Hall. At this meeting, he also told Hall, Pitts and other APS officials that he had "unsubstantiated information" that Waller had persuaded his staff to cheat on the 2006 Criterion-Referenced Competency Test.

"Everybody in the room heard me say that," Dukes testified.

Hall sat eating chicken wings and a salad during his presentation, he recalled. Her only question, Dukes said, was, "Do you have any more evidence?" Pitts stood up for Waller and noted Waller was relatively new to the job, Dukes recalled. "He was very supportive of Mr. Waller and the way he was running the operation over there."

Also present were former Human Resources Director Millicent Few, former Deputy Superintendent Kathy Augustine and Damaris Perryman-Garrett, who headed the office of internal resolution, Dukes said.

Few has pleaded guilty and is expected to testify. Her plea agreement says that while she does not have an independent recollection of the May 10, 2006, meeting, she does not dispute Dukes' account of it.
Lawson questioned Dukes about the APS central office's visitors' log from that day. It showed Dukes signed in at 11:25 a.m. It also indicated Dukes was signed out at 11:47 a.m.

During his testimony, Dukes said his meeting with Hall lasted the better part of an hour or longer than an hour. He said he had no explanation about the apparent discrepancy on the log and suggested someone else signed him out that day, putting in the incorrect time.

Lawson also noted that another person had signed in at 11:17 a.m. that same day and signed out at 3:44 p.m. Moreover, this person said he was meeting with Hall and Augustine, while Dukes wrote that he was meeting with Perryman-Garrett, Lawson said.

Dukes said he wrote that he was meeting with the internal affairs director because he first went to her office on the third floor before both of them took the elevator up to Hall's office on the eighth floor.

When asked by Rucker how certain he was that he met with Hall, Pitts and the others, Dukes said, "100 percent."

After Dukes stepped down, Rucker called Dwynell Williams, who runs a catering business and told jurors she brought lunch to Hall's conference room at 11 a.m. on the date in question.

Williams' log from that day showed she brought "2 meats," "salad" and other food and beverages. At least one of the meat items was certainly chicken, Williams testified, although she made no mention of chicken wings.

This lack of specificity prompted defense attorney Gerald Griggs, who represents former teacher Pamela Williamson, to jump up and ask Williams a single question.

"How many ways can you prepare chicken?" he asked.

"Why, 50 ways," Williams replied.

Cheating was not the only crime in this case. The incredible amount of taxpayer dollars spent on the separate investigations alone was probably extreme. There were several investigations conducted into the APS case. It began with the red flag out of Deerwood Academy. Students who overwhelmingly failed the spring Criterion-Referenced Competency Tests (CRCT) passed the summer retake with "suspiciously remarkable test score gains on the CRCT summer math retest," says the DA's office. Prosecutors claimed, "The erasure analysis revealed a statistically improbable high number of wrong-to-right changes indicating that cheating occurred at Deerwood." The test company, CTB/McGraw Hill, conducted the examination of the wrong-to-right erasures for the entire state, and the excessively high erasures raised flags everywhere. The Governor's Office for Student

Achievement (GOSA) gave districts with flags a chance to do an internal investigation. This led APS to form the Blue Ribbon Commission (BRC), which was made up of the Atlanta Chamber of Commerce community partners, the APS central office staff, and attorneys from King & Spalding. When the BRC report turned out to be a joke, Governor Sonny Perdue of Georgia appointed the Georgia Bureau of Investigation (GBI). The governor found the BRC report "to be woefully inadequate." I remember reading an article in which the governor was quoted as saying, "It was a sad day in Atlanta." Finally, the DA's office did an additional investigation before indicting the case four years after the scandal initially broke.

Everyone knows how multiple-choice testing sheets work. What most people, including educators didn't know, was that these bubble sheets indicated more than right or wrong answers. The media reports that it was CTB/McGraw Hill, the maker of the test, which reported to GOSA that the 2009 CRCT test was mishandled. In 2010, Georgia's governor quickly revealed what they learned from the test maker as a result of the 2009 test. After comparing the wrong-to-right (WTR) erasures by grade, test subject, and class to the average for the state, CTB/McGraw Hill determined, "The results of the erasure analysis showed that in thirty-five Georgia school districts, including APS, a significant number of classes had WTR erasures that were dramatically and disconcertingly higher than the state average."

When the erasure analysis was released, I received a call from my executive director, who informed me that Parks Middle School had an extremely high erasure rate. His response to me was, "It looks like something's going wrong over there," or "Something is going on over there." It was a long time ago, but that was the gist of his statement. I'm not sure how long the district had the information, but once the erasure analysis was released, Pitts notified me about two days prior to the story making the front page of the *Atlanta Journal–Constitution*. There was no sense of urgency until it became a media matter.

I will never forget that we had a scheduled principals' meeting at Booker T. Washington High School one day after the release of the erasure analysis. What was unusual that day was that there was a different atmosphere in the principals' meeting, and Dr. Hall was present. Dr. Hall was not always present at principals' meetings, but she was present that day, and she was first to speak. After she spoke, she departed to go tend to some other so-called "urgent matters." Her departure stood out as much as her presence.

When she spoke, she talked about all of the school reforms that have gone on in the district. Maybe she was trying to sell us or sell herself on our work. I didn't understand her stance at that point, but I can now remember reiterating those reforms as I defended myself before finally coming clean. She wanted us, if asked, to be able to lay out for anyone how our school reforms caused the score increases. She stressed best practices, "working on the work," implementing best teaching strategies at a high level. The she went for the trump card. She spoke emotionally about what it meant to be educators in a district that served a predominantly black community, and how sometimes others didn't think that black children could even learn. She consistently spoke about the possibilities of the education in the black community.

It kind of shifted from a principals' meeting to a mini pep rally. I surmise that at this point, most everybody in the room knew what had been going on throughout the district. It was impossible for me to believe then, and even more impossible now, to think she may not have known. She should have known. She knew, which is why she needed the pep rally in order to tell us to "continue on the work to keep implementing school reforms at high levels." Again, hindsight says "reforms at high levels" was an innuendo for "if you keep on cheating, we will be fine." But she did not condone cheating in that meeting; she did not even use the word "cheating" in her presentation. She only talked about the work and black children being able to learn and the school reforms that had been in place to help the children reach high levels. Dr. Hall had better coded language than the best street gangs.

At the end of her presentation or pep rally or her motivational speech, she walked out of the room, leaving the principals with the feeling like it was all under control, with the feeling that she had it all handled. "Keep working on the work, don't be distracted," is what she said. Now I think that could be interpreted as, "Don't worry about what I will be doing over here to save myself, you just keep doing what you have been doing." Even though she tried to paint a picture of business as usual, most of us in that meeting knew it wasn't business as usual, and I am sure that there were others like myself that understood the chickens had just come home to roost.

I remember having a conversation with a colleague and asking him about what he was going to do, and his response was "I'm going to wait it out. What are you going to do?" And I replied, the same. I think at some point we all hoped, especially initially, that whatever it was would pass over. We were not the only district with wrong-to-right erasures. However, we seemed to have been the only district that received so much criticism, media attention, prosecution, and punishment.

Once Dr. Hall finished with the pep rally in the principals' meeting, she departed the building, and we began to work on that day's agenda. Assistant Superintendent of Instruction Kathy Augustine never commented on any of it at that point. She just led us through the business of the day.

After that principals' meeting, we started receiving other trainings that I understand now why they were so important. One of the major trainings that I remember receiving was how to deal with and handle the media. It was a very extensive training, how not to avoid them, not to discuss major issues. We were only to talk about the progress of the schools and the districts, and to rely heavily upon the implementation of school reforms and implementation at high levels. We were basically taught how to steer clear from any accusations, from being boxed in by the media, and from looking like we were running from cameras. We were taught how to try to shape the conversation with the media into an APS moment of advertisement. I didn't understand why that was so important then, but as the days passed, I began to understand why it was important.

While the teachers and administrators were in meetings and trainings, the Blue Ribbon Commission was formed.

By now, the climate is hostile, morale is low, people are nervous. It was at that point I am sure teaching reached an all-time low. The rumors were spreading, and discussions of a witch hunt were swirling. Now teachers who had not been involved with or had no knowledge of cheating prior to the erasure report had reason to be concerned and started seeking answers of their own inside of their schools. No one trusted anyone.

In February 2010, there was a reception at the exclusive 191 Commerce Club to welcome the new CEO of the Atlanta Education Fund (AEF). Established before my time in APS, the AEF is a private group of business and civic leaders that was created to support Atlanta's public schools. John Rice, the former CEO, said the AEF would be launching an independent investigation into the eraser analysis the governor's office had just released.

By August of the same year that the irregularities were revealed, Dr. Hall had compiled a team and completed what she says was a thorough investigation. The commission was charged with finding out why there were so many wrong-to-right erasures, as if there would have been another answer other than test tampering. Based on the subsequent interview by the GBI of Dr. Hall and news reports, the superintendent had a heavy hand in the BRC and their findings.

The AEF contacted the powerful business owners in the city via the Atlanta Chamber of Commerce. According to Dr. Hall, the AEF and the Chamber of Commerce would both help conduct the investigation and help pay for it. It is unclear to me how much the Chamber of Commerce was directly involved, if at all, but Gary Price who chaired the BRC was also a member of the Chamber of Commerce. Other players on the commission included the school board president and other people with direct interest in keeping the cover-up going.

Dr. Hall reached out to her contacts and eventually recommended to the independent BRC that the statistical analysis to determine if cheating occurred be done by Caveon. The Caveon website describes their services as

... state-of-the-art test security and test item development services dedicated to detecting, correcting, and preventing test fraud. . . . [Caveon] identifies breaches, offers remedies to stop and prosecute abuses, and provides prevention services to help secure your testing program from further compromise.

Hall said an unnamed consultant from the Bill and Melinda Gates Foundation recommended Caveon after other testing companies refused. ETS, the distributor of the widely known SAT test, was said to turn down the BRC's request to handle the investigation. Hall also included KPMG in the Blue Ribbon Commission. KPMG is a nationally recognized forensic accounting firm that was recommended by GOSA. Given the formation of the BRC and having a highly recommended testing company lined up, Dr. Hall says she stepped aside and let them do their work.

Once the BRC report was released, an emergency board meeting took place during which preliminary findings were discussed. I always wondered the purpose of the BRC report. Was it to really seek the truth or to see where everyone would stand if there were another investigation to come down? Unfortunately, hindsight has not proven to be completely helpful in this case. With the high-profile arrest and trial, all of the truth has still not come to light, despite multiple investigations. I now believe Dr. Hall knew that things were going to get worse. She hoped the political power interested in our schools looking like top performers would help sell the BRC report and put the speculation of cheating to bed. But I also believe she needed to know who would rat out her and her team. She wanted to know who knew what, so she could start on her exit strategy. The BRC investigation would help her to get answers to lots of those questions.

Statements and comments made by teachers, administrators, and staff during the BRC investigation totally contradicted the comments and statements they had made under oath to the GBI. But I guess there are bound to be a difference in the stories when you compare a twenty-page in-house report to the four-hundred-page GBI report and the six-month criminal trial. The truth for most folks isn't in a memoir however, but I'm sure for most it can be found somewhere in between each of those investigations.

The questioning began when the BRC was formed and the attorneys were hired. We were told that if we did not participate in the investigations that we would be terminated for insubordination. No educator wants to be terminated for insubordination, so everyone began to cooperate with this initial investigation. It wasn't until after the indictment that we really learned that this, too, was a clever ploy by Dr. Hall to protect her district secret. But as I will discuss later, Dr. Hall didn't listen to her own statements at the pep rally. Just as our district was being picked on because it had black students, a majority black school district is not privy to the same outcomes in court. In the pretrial hearings, a major motion involving Garrity rights was argued. These rights protect public employees from being forced to incriminate themselves if their employers are conducting an investigation. Dr. Hall had insisted that all APS employees cooperate or be terminated. The defense attorneys argued her stance was illegal, according to a US Supreme Court decision from the 1960s. At the time of writing this memoir, the APS cheating scandal Garrity motion was making its way up to the Georgia Supreme Court while the trial was ongoing, which means the defendants lost the motion at the trial level. Hall and the attorneys on my team who did not see racial issues the way I did in this case were surprised to see this long-standing case law didn't work to dismiss our case. In 2018, the teachers lost this appeal and their sentences were upheld.

During the initial investigation, many of us did what we had been trained to do the past several weeks prior to the BRC appointment and investigation. We controlled the conversation in the room by referring to our implementation of school reforms at high levels. We pivoted the conversation toward reassuring everyone in the room that children would learn and could learn if taught properly and the proper resources were provided.

The BRC questioned several people in the district, but I was questioned twice. One of the major problems was that for me personally, even though I knew what had been going on in the district and at Parks Middle School, I still had a lot of questions about what happened in 2009. I still do not understand specifically why the 2009 erasures were so high at Parks. They were so high that Parks Middle School had the highest number of wrong-to-right erasures when the GBI ranked the schools. As a part of the investigation, the BRC interviewed more than 290 people at APS, many at Parks. From the interviews, the BRC indicated that the teachers at Parks knew nothing about cheating. They extrapolated from the lack of "whistle-blowers" that cheating had not occurred at Parks. I know cheating took place every year in question, except 2009, at Parks. If nothing else, the BRC's lack of finding supported the need for continued investigation by GOSA. I know from my own experience that the investigation that was paid for by the BRC did not contain all of the information that was needed in this case.

I hesitate to make presumptions about 2009 because I was not privy to all the information. I did not actively participate in the administration of the CRCT in 2009. That was the year my goddaughter died in the car accident, the same goddaughter whose trial was conducted by the Fulton DA's office. That was the same trial that led me to hire my legal team. I was helping make funeral arrangements for my goddaughter who had died in the car accident. I was not in the building, so I can't personally say what happened during the 2009 CRCT testing. Had the scores not caused the investigations, I may have eventually found out. But I never did, and I am left to speculate, like I am with many issues in this case. In my plea deal, I talked about it being by then a machine that would have worked with or without me. Today as I sit and reflect, I don't know if there was a machine that would have worked with or without me. I'm not sure. By machine, I mean an organized system that once started automatically resulted in a particular outcome.

The BRC issued a twenty-two-page report that in summary said there were changes that need to be made, explanations for the test irregularities, but no evidence of widespread cheating in APS. There is no wonder that the governor stepped in. It also helps to show my belief that Dr. Hall knew that more scrutiny was coming no matter how the commission acted. Therefore, I believe the self-appointed BRC became her investigation into who was still on the team. I believe it was a "dry run" for a full investigation. I believe that the real purpose of the commission was to find out how Dr. Hall could clear her own name. I believed then, and I think others did, too, that if Dr. Hall was cleared we would all be cleared.

The report said:

> *The security analysis of written APS testing policies and procedures indicated a "tight" testing environment, which could be improved, but which did not contain significant security policy gaps, although the BRC's investigative team found that there were inconsistencies in the application of testing policies and procedures.*
>
> *Neither the erasure analysis nor the traditional investigation revealed any data or other evidence that there was any district wide or centrally coordinated effort to manipulate the 2009 CRCT scores and outcomes of students in the 58 APS schools. Additionally, there were no self-admissions by any central office staff, district office staff or school staff of any wrongdoing in connection with the 2009 CRCT.*
>
> *Caveon was not able to determine the statistical probability of a student's answering a question on the 2009 CRCT test correctly based on his or her level of proficiency in the subject being tested due to limited access to all test answer sheets and item (test question) level data. An examination of this data could have indicated the probability that a student would change his or her answers from WTR based on his or her*

responses to questions within the subject (i.e. getting hard questions right while getting easy questions wrong).

Notwithstanding these limitations, the Investigative Team was able to conclude that base on the strength of the data that was available and analyzed, coupled with the information gained through the traditional investigation, the results and findings of the Investigative team reported to the BRC would not have been materially different.

One of my favorite quotes from the BRC report is particularly telling. Nothing in the original CTB/McGraw Hill report of irregularities pointed fingers at teachers, students, or the central office. Yet the BRC report was very clear in that there was not any "centrally coordinated" cheating:

The investigative team did not find any data or other evidence, nor were there qualified allegations made, that there was any district wide or centrally coordinated effort to manipulate the 2009 CRCT scores and outcomes of students in the 58 APS schools.

Caveon, the audit group specially picked by Dr. Hall also determined, "Current written APS testing policies and procedures are well defined and established a strong framework for a highly controlled testing environment from receipt to return of tests to the state." The bold statements were repeated as boldly as the mantras taught to the teachers during the Dr. Hall pep rally. Without demanding it and despite her small five-foot stature, Dr. Hall had a way of getting you to sing the same tune. Also interesting to note, Caveon created the Caveon Index, a complex system of characteristics that helped them to rank trouble schools to be referred back to APS for further internal investigation. In the Caveon Index evaluation, Parks was number nine of twelve schools with some concerns. In the later GBI investigation, Parks was listed as number one based on the excessively high erasures in 2009.

In its suggestions for improvement, the BRC again tipped its hand and what would later become an obvious truth, there was a "culture of cheating" within APS. Of course, the BRC watered down this mention of the culture by more eloquently suggesting APS

. . . drive culture change throughout the district to create an environment that effectively balances attention to measurable student outcomes with attention to positive, ethical behavior. Proactively reassess incentive systems and performance evaluation processes for all district employees with a focus on achieving this appropriate balance.

The BRC's final remarks were likely the most interesting of them all. The commission appointed itself and APS as the leader in cheating or as they stated it, "The 2009 CRCT erasure investigation results offer APS the opportunity to take the lead in establishing best in class test security practices." Who better to instruct the rest of the country on how to catch cheating in schools than the district who took it to the next level?

Chapter 4

Last Day at Parks—First Day of Reality

The BRC report did result in actual action by APS. It was then when true emotion would kick in for me. Prior to that, I was still "riding it out" with my colleagues. I had no clue what would happen, but I also internally suspected that if the rumors about APS investigating itself via the BRC was true, then not much could go wrong.

When the BRC report was complete, there was an emergency board meeting for all principals. Some principals—myself included— were notified about four hours prior to the board meeting that we would need to meet with Dr. Augustine, the deputy superintendent of APS at the time, after the meeting. Dr. Augustine had worked under Dr. Hall in New Jersey and had moved with her in her same role when Dr. Hall was hired by APS. She was the only direct line of communications to and from Dr. Hall. Since all projects went through her, she reported the yeas or nays from Dr. Hall. Dr. Augustine was known as the "godmother" of the school district, but she was not among the people indicted in 2014.

While the BRC investigation was being released to the public in 2011, Dr. Augustine jumped ship. She was selected as the superintendent for the De Soto School District right outside of Dallas, Texas. After only one day on her new job at the beginning of the 2011– 2012 school year, Dr. Augustine was put on administrative leave based on the reports on the cheating scandal at APS. The DeSoto School

District gave her one year's salary as severance, which meant she received around $157,000 to get her out of the school system that selected her based on the improvements made in Atlanta.

Prior to meeting with Dr. Augustine and the other principals, Michael Pitts, the executive director of School Reform Team 2, told me that he didn't understand why I was at the meeting. My name had not been on the original reassignment list. Since the BRC listed Parks so far down their concern list, in addition to some executive office maneuvering, Pitts thought I would be in the clear. His statement made it evident there had been a discussion of who was going to be reassigned based on the issues in his or her school.

Only the principals being reassigned met that night. The SRTs, school-based teams that meet regularly to discuss strategies and provide support for students, were called to Dunbar Elementary. Dr. Augustine called all the principals individually to make them aware of the upcoming reassignments. The next day, we met in her conference room. We were told that there were problems with our schools, and we were being put on official notice. Dr. Augustine placed copies of the BRC report on the table; its appendix stated who said what, when, and where. If anyone made a statement that indicated cheating, it was listed by first and last name. It gave me the perception that the BRC's objective was to find out who was on the team and who was not. I believe Hall and Augustine knew that instinctively people would go into preservation mode and try to neutralize or bully the people who snitched or gave up information. Although the BRC report did not have a whole lot to say about what went on at Parks, I was one of the administrators being reassigned. Another hint to me, in hindsight, Dr. Hall knew that further investigations were coming. Although I was cleared by the internal investigation, the high number of erasures at Parks would come out eventually and need to be addressed.

After that meeting, things moved quickly. On the day that Pitts hosted a mandatory staff development session, I was in Toccoa, Georgia, preaching at an annual conference. Ironically, in the middle of the drama unfolding in APS and the uncertainty about what would happen to me, my sermon was entitled "Don't Throw in the Towel."

After I had delivered my sermon at the conference, I noticed that I had several missed calls from Pitts, several principals, and from another APS phone number, which I later found out to be Dunbar Elementary School.

I listened to my voice mails before calling anyone back. I learned that I specifically was going to be reassigned, and Dr. Augustine wanted to talk to me personally. I called into the main office to let them know that I was on my way from Elberton, about a two-hour drive. Dr. Augustine waited for me at Dunbar Elementary. Upon my arrival, she informed me that I was being reassigned to the APS central office. She could not give me any details. But she ordered me to go back to Parks, have a faculty meeting, make sure that everything was in place for the opening of school, and prepare to start reporting to work at the central office the following workday.

I did as I was instructed. I went back to Parks and called a faculty meeting. By then, most teachers knew that all the principals had been reassigned. At the faculty meeting, I acknowledged the rumors and informed them that I was being reassigned. I told my faculty that we did expect them to keep working and to have a good opening of the school year.

We were not given a time frame on how long we would be reassigned. During the faculty meeting, Pitts informed us that he was coming over to assist at Parks. During the meeting, I specifically asked the teachers: "Is there anybody who knows anything about cheating?" Complete silence. I wanted to know if anybody would admit to cheating at Parks since the BRC report did not contain any evidence of cheating at the school. With the BRC report as the basis for changes, I suspected someone or something else was the cause. I waited to see if anyone would be so bold. Part of me knew they would not, and a silent room would reinforce that despite this sudden change, the plan was to keep the story the same. No cheating occurred at Parks Middle School.

When Pitts came over to talk to the staff, he told them that some other investigation would probably take place. He told the staff not to start changing their story or they were going to get themselves in trouble. Although subsequent reports suggest that I was the one who had told teachers to stick to the script during that meeting, that was not the case. Nor had Pitts and I discussed keeping people in line with their original stories. But that was the way it worked in APS. That was the culture, the ethos in the Atlanta Public Schools. At first, the common goal was to keep the schools open for the kids in the community by skewing the test numbers while we educated them the best we could. Now the common goal was to keep our butts out of the pot that was starting to boil. But no one discussed the common goal. They didn't need to. The solution was implicit in the problem.

One thing I have always been certain of is that this cheating culture existed at Parks long before I arrived, and it would have continued whether I or anyone else would have taken over as principal of that school in 2006. I think Pitts knew from my first day at Parks Middle School that there would be some teachers who hated my guts for no reason, before they even knew me. It was personal, because Dr. Hall fired Michael Simms. The teachers had been comfortable with him as their principal, and the cheating culture was safe with him there. Whoever would have come and sat in that chair at Parks Middle School was bound to be tied up in something. Not to say all principals would have succumb to the temptation to participate in cheating, but without a doubt, if not cheating, then some other scandal would have eventually rose to the top. It is no coincidence that all of the teachers who willingly participated in cheating with me were handpicked and hired by Simms before I was hired. It was those teachers who initially gave me the most trouble from the day I stepped foot in the door.

The relationship in which this culture of cheating is based is deeper than employer-employee. Simms had built loyalty on his staff through a series of favors. For example, he hired Damian Northern who had been sleeping in his car until Simms gave him the position to teach social studies. He purchased a car for another down-and-out teacher, Damany Lewis, who taught math. According to Lewis, Simms had brought a car to Lewis's house and told him, "I need you to clean this car up for me, detail it, clean it up real good for me, and call me when you're finished." After Lewis cleaned up the car, he called Simms and told him the car was ready. Then Simms told him, "Good, keep it, and drive it. It's for you."

The rest of Simms's team didn't need gifts or favors. Their loyalty had begun prior to Simms becoming the principal at Parks. Kelly Smith is Simms's cousin. She was hired as a social studies teacher in the district because of her family connection. The bookkeeper, Ms. Marshall, is Simms's godmother. She grew up as best friends with Simms's mother. Simms had picked Stacey Webb to be the math facilitator at the school, despite not having a math teaching certificate. Webb caused tons of problems since she was supposed to be able to teach math teachers how to teach math and didn't have the qualifications to do so. Webb was very close to Simms as they all were. Crystal Draper was included in this crew. She came from the Fulton County Schools and was later hired by Simms to teach social studies.

Because these people were loyal to Simms for many different reasons, they fought me from day one. During the faculty meeting, in which all of Simms's team attended, I think Pitts was telling them I know where some of your loyalties lie. He was warning them in that non-direct APS way, "Don't be in here saying stuff, making up stuff." It later came out that those teachers who were on Simms's team made formal and informal complaints about me. His warning was direct: "Don't start saying stuff now; you'll get your own self in trouble." Pitts drew a clear picture that now that teachers had made statements that no cheating occurred, if they made another statement contrary to the first, the inconsistency will point to their own secrets. I also believe Pitts was also singing the mantra from the main office that we would weather the storm. Whether he actually believed what he was selling or was as clueless as the rest of us, only Pitts can tell you now. At the time of writing this memoir, Pitts was one of the defendants still on trial. In

2015, he was convicted and sentenced to three years in jail with seven years to follow on probation.

Part of what made it so difficult to take responsibility in the beginning was the difficulty I had with Simms's team. I truly felt then, and still do now, that I was set up. It didn't help that the teachers acted in a way that gave me reason to believe that and hone in on those hints. In the faculty meeting, Draper yelled out, "Why can't Mr. Reid be the principal?" That statement still puzzles me today. Gregory Reid, the assistant principal at Parks, had been on twenty-three interviews to become a principal. Despite his best efforts, he had not made it out of the assistant principal role. He had become anxious about becoming a principal. Draper's statement, among others, makes me believe the plan was to get me out so they could get someone they preferred in the principal's chair. It's one of the many reasons why the 2009 test, when I wasn't in the school, was a red flag that put Parks at the top of the cheating list. I believe that although the teachers who were hired under Simms had become a part of my cheating team, I was still not their favorite. By cheating excessively, the red flags would go up to get me out and they could lobby for the principal they preferred.

As I sit and reflect today, I still wonder if this may have been an opportunity for people to point their finger at the cheating taking place. I wonder if the cause of CTB/McGraw Hill getting information from GOSA or vice versa came out of Parks. From where I sat, cheating in 2009 was not necessary. There should not have been a need for so many erasures because the kids at that point were able to probably stand on their own and pass the tests. I even believe the majority would have exceeded, at a minimum in reading and language arts. That makes me believe that Parks was a pawn. Someone cheated excessively that year to have me ousted or maybe put APS on blast. The previous reports having gone ignored, excessive cheating that could be detected needed to be pushed.

Because we taught along the way, there should have been less erasing to meet targets. The longer we were in place to work with the children, the higher their scores should have gone. We had students coming from all over the city not just the area around the school, which gave us higher-performing students. We had best practices in place to make sure our neighborhood kids were doing great. There just should have been less erasing as time went forward not more.

In 2009, I remember coming in to school to get something out of my office and to finish up some paperwork before I went to my godchild's funeral. The testing coordinator approached me to sign off on the tests. I remember him being very jovial and laughing as I walked by the office. As I was about to exit the building, he caught me right by the secretary's desk and said, "Doc, I need you to sign off on the tests." I asked him, as I had asked him every single year, if "there were any testing improprieties reported to him that he would like to report to me," and he said no. I signed off on the tests. Afterward, I found out the tests were being turned in late because he had been waiting for me to sign off on them.

I left the building, and very honestly speaking, I didn't think any more about it. I should not have been asked to sign off on the tests because I was not present for the administration of the tests. Since hindsight is twenty/twenty, I probably should not have signed off on the tests that year.

After Draper raised the question at the meeting about Reid not becoming the principal at Parks, Pitts told everyone that Assistant Principal Reid was under investigation as well as the whole school.

At the end of the meeting, Damien Northern ran out, kicking the walls like he always did. He threw a classic temper tantrum, kicking the walls, hitting the walls, and basically giving himself away to anyone who otherwise had no clue who may have been involved. Damany Lewis ran out behind him to comfort him because they were friends. Lewis would later tell others that I instructed him to not only cheat, but I gave him the instructions to do all types of things. Lewis said he went after Northern at my request, but that is not true. They were friends.

My ego made me wonder why Northern would have that emotional outburst about my reassignment when I knew he didn't like me. In hindsight, now that I've had time to reflect, it wasn't because I was being reassigned, it was because the plan they had in place to oust me and put Reid in as the principal didn't quite work out the way they had planned. At this time of intense district scrutiny, having another principal in place would make it impossible to hide their past activity.

After the meeting and tantrums were over, I went to my office, gathered a few things, and tidied up some stuff to make sure the office would be presentable for whoever would take the lead of the school. I didn't pack, because I didn't know that I would be gone forever. I just thought the storm would pass over in a couple of weeks and that we would be back at work to work. I left everything as it was. I continued as if it would be business as usual. That is how I felt. I left instructions on the desk for stuff that was done or needed to be done. I did a walk-through of the building to make sure that it was ready for the opening of school, and it was. Then I walked out of the doors of the school. I was not sad. I was not anxious. I felt like a load had been lifted off of me the second I walked outside of those doors. It was that moment I felt as if I would never walk in those doors again.

Chapter 5

Reassigned

The next week, I began working in the central office on middle school transformation. My desk was in a closet that had been converted to office space. The space was also occupied by another principal, Lisa Smith, who had been placed under investigation in 2008 for cheating at her school—Deerwood Elementary. Just like Smith, I had been reassigned along with all of the other suspected principals. It became very difficult and depressing to go to work and sit in that little enclosed space. It felt like I had academic leprosy. Everyone looked at me as if I were the scum of the earth. People had conversations about me while I was sitting there. In reality, they were talking about the whole scandal, but in that moment, I thought it was all about me, and all their information was wrong. After going from nonstop busy days to having to sit there and not have enough to keep my mind occupied and busy was torture in and of itself. For me, it was punishment. Every single day in that small office, I was anxious about the future. This type of anxiety will give you time to convince yourself you were right all along. Then it gave you time to convince yourself that you can get other people to buy your story.

In hindsight, I think they wanted us thirteen principals to be together throughout this process. The Atlanta Public Schools administration hoped that we would build a bond and maybe build loyalty to one another. That loyalty would serve Dr. Hall and Dr. Augustine to give them a chance at being completely shielded from being accused of wrongdoing. We were put in the central office and in those positions to keep us a part of the team so that we would not turn on the team but would rather stay with what we had been saying all the while.

Together we would, by circumstance not because we were instructed, continue to work on the things we had been taught in our media preparatory class together. We were basically allowed to do whatever we wanted to do whenever we wanted. The only major difference that I can remember of accountability was the fact that we had to pay for parking downtown. Because of the circumstances, all thirteen of us tried to relate to one another. I know at least four or five of us downtown tried to make light of it and connect with one another by doing lunch every day or something else to get through the situation. No matter how light we attempted to make it in public, it was a tough time.

Because of the team approach, I was still confident it would all go away. I still believed it would be handled and dealt with seriously. But all the reassigned principals had come to the conclusion it wouldn't ever come down to anything serious or anything major, like criminal charges and a six-month trial. I think I had hoped that everyone else would have stuck to the script and say that no cheating had occurred. I didn't expect them to stick to their story for me because I knew that a lot of the people did not like me personally. But they did like their school. They were crazy about their school and the children there, and I thought they would hold up the information just for the sake of the school.

While I was reassigned, my sons were born. I remember taking time off. In retrospect, I should have taken more time off. I should have exhausted all of my time. But I didn't, I took a period of time off and went back to work. The only reason I think I did not resign at that point was my wife was pregnant and I needed the health insurance. That may have been the only reason I may have kept going to the central office every day. Every single day, going to that closet office, set up for depression, set up for misery. At that moment, I just felt like it was something I had to endure.

In the central office, I had more flexibility to accompany my reduced responsibility. I told my new executive director, Crystal Lottig, that I would like to change my work schedule from eight to four to nine to five because I wanted to start taking my daughter to school. That was something I could not do as a principal. I had to be at school to receive other people's children, so I never had a chance to take my own daughter to school her entire school career.

I remember the first day I took her to school. I looked in the back seat and said, "Baby, how old are you again?" She had grown up on me that quick. While I was raising everybody else's children, my own child was not being raised by her father. To this day, I still take my daughter to school.

From AJC.com

Ex-principal accuses APS supervisor in cheating scandal

Posted: 7:25 p.m. Monday, Dec. 1, 2014
By Bill Rankin and Ty Tagami The Atlanta Journal-Constitution

Christopher Waller, the "poster child" for the Atlanta Public Schools testing scandal, testified Monday he orchestrated cheating at Parks Middle School and then kept quiet about it at the direction of superiors.

Waller freely admitted orchestrating cheating on standardized tests over a four-year period when he served as principal at Parks Middle. He also told jurors that when questions about cheating surfaced, the message from his direct supervisor was loud and clear: keep your mouth shut.

With a touch of nostalgia, if not irony, Waller took the stand wearing a black sweater vest with the Parks Middle School emblem over his heart that included the slogan "Eliminating The Achievement Gap."

Waller provided testimony against Michael Pitts, a former School Reform Team executive director and one of a dozen former educators on trial. Pitts ignored Waller's suspicions of test cheating at feeder elementary schools and threatened to make things more difficult if Waller wouldn't stop talking about it, Waller testified.

Before a wrong-to-right erasure analysis flagged more classrooms at Parks for suspiciously high test scores than any other school in the state, Parks was celebrated by then-Superintendent Beverly Hall as a model for student achievement.

"It's no secret I was the poster child" for student achievement, Waller testified. "Dr. Hall promoted me, she lauded me. She held me up as a banner, a flag. . . . Consequently, I also became the poster child for the Atlanta Public Schools test-cheating scandal."

Waller was among 35 defendants indicted in the test-cheating scandal, charged with racketeering and four other felonies. In February, he pleaded guilty to a single felony count—false statements and writings. He was sentenced to five years on probation, ordered to perform 1,000 hours of community service and *required to pay $50,000 in court costs, fines and restitution. He also agreed to testify for the prosecution.*

Waller continues his testimony Tuesday with Pitts' lawyer, George Lawson, conducting his cross-examination. . . .

Waller, an ordained minister, joined the Atlanta school system in February 2005. At age 32, he was the youngest principal in the district.

At the time, Parks was at risk of closure for having repeatedly failed to meet Adequate Yearly Progress, a benchmark for student achievement based largely on standardized test scores. It also failed to meet the even-more demanding APS test targets, meaning Parks's staff was consigned to the bleachers at the school district's annual convocation. "It was almost like having leprosy," Waller said of the humiliating experience.

Subsequently, Waller summoned his assistant principal and reading coach and told them the school could not meet test targets. "I knew that we were in trouble," Waller testified.

It was during that conversation when an agreement was reached to use "human intervention" to change test answers, Waller said. From 2006 to 2009, rampant cheating occurred at Parks, often when Waller took the school's testing coordinator out to long lunches while teachers gained access to answer sheets and made corrections.

Waller said his school would never meet the targets because students from the feeder schools, such as Gideons Elementary and Dunbar Elementary, were performing far below grade level even though they had scored well on standardized tests. Some of these students had exceeded expectations on their Criterion-Referenced Competency Test, he said.

Waller said he told Pitts that this showed cheating had to be going on at the elementary school level.

But Pitts told his principal to stop "slandering" elementary school teachers, Waller testified. If Waller refused to stop talking about it, Pitts warned, Parks would receive only the "lowest-performing kids" from the feeder schools, Waller testified.

Waller said he got the message.
"I closed my mouth," he testified. "It wasn't helping. It was actually hurting."

On another occasion, when Pitts and Waller walked through Parks, they saw a student who was misbehaving because he couldn't keep up with his class's reading lesson, Waller said.

"That's one of your 'exceeds kids' from Gideons," Waller said he told Pitts.

Pitts just "laughed the way he laughed" and then said, "Sometimes kids just test well," Waller testified.

Waller explained to jurors: "Just not having a good test day and not being able to read are two different things."

Test-cheating at Parks became glaringly apparent in 2008 when almost all of the school's seventh-grade students had perfect standardized science test scores, Waller said.

Pitts told Waller to call Lester McKee, the APS research, planning and accountability director, Waller said. During the call, McKee said, "(Expletive) happens and sometimes when it happens, it's not always bad. Let's see if anyone else says something," Waller testified.

Waller said he called Pitts back and relayed what McKee had told him. "(Pitts) told me to keep my mouth shut and let's see what happens," Waller testified.

Later, when asked if Parks's students had been cheated, Waller said, "I've struggled with that question. . . . There was cheating at Parks, but I'm not ready to say the children were cheated."

Waller acknowledged his school lost out on federal funding earmarked for low-achieving students but said private grants helped pay for supplemental learning, such as martial arts, tutorials, music lessons and out-of-state trips for students.

Waller did, however, admit to "a moral lapse in judgment."

"It wasn't the right thing to do," he said. "At the time, I had no concept I was hurting anyone. . . . I had no concept it could be construed to be criminal. I know differently today."

Chapter 6

Stick to the Lie!

Initially, the posture I took was whatever I said in the first investigation would remain my script throughout every investigation. My plan was to stick to my lie. I continued to deny that I had any knowledge of the erasures, which was not true. I stuck to the script that I never told teachers to cheat, and that was true. We're getting into technicalities but technically, I never told or asked a teacher to cheat. So, I continued to deny that I had told teachers to cheat. And I denied there was cheating at Parks Middle School. Part of my script I learned from Dr. Hall at the principals' meeting and during our media training sessions. The script said that all black children could learn, and they did learn. My script highlighted that we have evidence to show that all black children can learn. I left out of the script, however, that they just couldn't learn fast enough to keep up with the targets.

Holding that shell around the cheating scandal made me turn the scandal into a purely personal attack. So, I started to create a whole list of reasons why I was right and "they" were wrong. I was upset that no one was talking about what had really happened at Parks, so instead I made up defenses.

Defense 1: I felt a fair discussion should include the good works we did at Parks.

Defense 2: We can't ignore the fact cheating began in Parks's feeder elementary schools, which were also steeped in the cheating culture. We had to cheat to keep up.

Defense 3: Principal Simms's crew was intentionally fueling a lot of attention toward Parks Middle School by excessive cheating to get me fired.

Defense 4: Several teachers lied about how the cheating occurred. People who I never spoke to about cheating said that I asked them to cheat, and that's not quite the way that it rolled out.

Defense 5: I understood the form that I signed asking whether or not there had been any improprieties reported in testing to only refer to the "reporting." No improprieties had been "reported" to me during the years in question. It's a technicality. I may have known, but cheating was not reported.

Defense 6: They did an analysis on wrong-to-right erasures, but didn't include in the evaluation, right to wrong. This would have statistically brought down the value of the number of changes significantly, showing erasing wasn't that rampant. I believe it shows the children did earn some of those correct answers.

My defense counsel had to break down each one, a couple of times, to convince me that the defenses of *they did it first, it was a conspiracy,* and *yes, I cheated but I did not kick the dog* would not fly. As to Defense 1, LaDawn said the law does not grade on a scale. You don't get an A for effort, and there are no bonus points for extra credit projects. The fact that we taught kids and took them on trips, too, could be presented to the jury, but that was not the issue before a jury to decide.

At my request, LaDawn met with Warren and Linda Fortson, the education attorneys who had followed this case. They had been making the argument about the incorrect analysis based on right-to-wrong and wrong-to-right erasure analysis. LaDawn asked me, "How does the fact that the evaluation that led to the discovery of cheating was flawed matter if you know in fact cheating, as identified by the evaluation did occur?" Even after admitting my part, I felt it was an argument we should try at trial. The media exposure helped me to realize she was right. You could argue the proof of the erasures and a bad analysis only if you didn't have witnesses for the State of Georgia who have said, "Yes, I did erase."

Prior to the indictment, we speculated on all the potential charges the DA's office could pursue. It wasn't until after the indictment was finally presented that it was clear that my personal interpretation of the form, aka Defense 5, was a possible, albeit weak, defense to three of the five charges.

I would eventually enter a guilty plea to false statements and writings for willfully and falsely certifying that the Criterion-Referenced Competency Tests at Parks Middle School was properly and ethically administered. Yes, Defense 5 is a technicality argument, but our justice system is technical for a reason. I felt that we were signing off that no improprieties had been reported to us during that testing period. There was a process in the Examiner's Manual, and I told the teachers that the process required them to report improprieties to the testing coordinator. It was the testing coordinator's job to log in the report on the testing sheet. Teachers then needed to report the impropriety to me, and I would report it to my executive director who would tell me where to report it next. That never occurred while I was at Parks. The CRCT School Certification Form that we signed and swore to each year said:

(1) The written plans for testing were followed, including all directives in the Examiner's Manual, the Testing Coordinator's Manual, and system correspondence; and (2) There was ethical behavior on the part of all staff and all students involved in the test administration; any suspected testing irregularity/circumstance has been reported to the system coordinator.

There were no improprieties reported to me at all except for my last year as principal of Parks Middle School when there were several "irregularities or circumstances" reported. I was not in the building and did not have any discussions upon my return that directives were not followed and unethical behavior occurred in the administration of the test. I had convinced myself to make me feel mentally and emotionally secure, that as long as nothing was officially reported, that I was telling the truth when I swore to that form.

Looking back through the reports, I noted that Damany Lewis, a teacher from Simms's team said that Dr. Alfred Kiel, the testing coordinator at Parks, reported he could tell tests were moved around in his office because they were not the way he left them when he went out of the office. Lewis admitted to investigators and the grand jury that he took pictures of Dr. Kiel's office the next time he entered before moving the test. That way, when Lewis finished changing the answers, he was able to put everything else back where it was. No one discussed or worked directly with Dr. Kiel for cheating at Parks. To my knowledge, he was completely unaware. If Dr. Kiel noticed the change in his office, that would have been a clear testing impropriety. If Dr. Kiel made that statement to Lewis, then Dr. Kiel should have listed the impropriety on his test coordinator's sheet. The court discovery in the case shows that there were never any improprieties listed on the sheets for Parks for the years in question except 2009.

It finally got through to me, that even if everything I said in support of Defense 5 was true and accepted as reasonable to a jury, it was still not good enough to defend against the RICO charges that were indicted. After years of delay and after years of paying attorneys and being investigated, the indictment was issued just days before the statute of limitations ran out on some of the charges. We had waited four years for some clarity.

The legal team explained that even if the jury did not find I specifically did any of the actions listed in the indictment, if the jury thought I was a part of the overall conspiracy I would be found guilty. That is how RICO works. Just from being a part of the organization, even if you didn't know who else was involved, even if your part was small, even if your role was not illegal per se, if a person was involved in any way they were a part of the conspiracy. With Parks being the number one school in APS in erasures, it was becoming abundantly clear I was not going to be able to stick to my lie and come out of this situation without taking a serious chance of spending time in jail and away from my family.

I eventually realized that the words on the indictment didn't matter legally or morally because I had done something wrong. My participation in doing that wrong could allow a jury to find me criminally responsible. That's when I began to be very clear and transparent as to my part and the role that I played in the cheating scandal at Parks Middle School. Once I mentally decided that I was going to go forward and come clean, I decided that I would come clean with every question that was asked of me. I would answer every question very truthfully and I would not take the posture of protecting anyone other than me. I regret that I had not done that earlier.

When I finally did fess up to LaDawn, we had several more discussions that led me to finding my own words for what I did. It was not real until I was finally able to say out loud, "I orchestrated cheating at Parks Middle School on the 2006, 2007, and 2008 CRCT." When I said it the first time, I paused. Then I said it a few more times. It took several more discussions for me to say the words out loud describing my direct actions. LaDawn was patient with me by making me answer questions that pulled out the specific actions that were wrong.

The conversation in LaDawn's office started something like this:

LaDawn: Now that you have admitted you orchestrated cheating, what did you specifically do to orchestrate it?

Chris: You know . . . I led it. I knew it was going on. I did that. Yes. I did.

I was noncommittal but after longer discussion, I would come to be able to answer that question by giving details.

After I was told I needed to cheat to get our scores up by Dr. Hall's team, I met with Gregory Reid, Parks's assistant principal, and Sandra Ward, the reading coach at Parks. Together we laid out the plan that they would be the ones who would go out and communicate with the teachers directly. I would not be involved in that communication. I was to have plausible deniability. As the gatekeeper to the process of reporting cheating, if I didn't know, I didn't participate, then no one would get caught. In retrospect, I was protecting myself from having to ask any particular person to cheat. This is why I was stuck on Defense 4. The report that states I asked any teacher to cheat is a lie. At this point with all the truth I am telling, I have no reason to lie. What that means is the indictment, the investigations, and the witch hunt were based on a wrong analysis of erasures topped off by teachers who were lying to save their own behinds. Teachers were told, during several of the investigations, if you just come clean, you won't be prosecuted. With the exception of the Blue Ribbon Commission report, at each stage, teachers told more and more lies to the investigators and media while simultaneously admitting cheating on their own behalf.

I am not surprised because the purpose of all the investigations was to determine if there was "system-wide" or "system-led" cheating. That is the prosecutor's basis for the RICO charge. At each stage, investigators pushed through questions and innuendo to get direct information that proved cheating by all those suspected. Damany Lewis had fingered me, but then he had to back it up with direct proof.

"Mr. Waller was never in the building when I changed the answers, and I never had a direct conversation with him about those changes," would not fly for the aggressive investigators who had the truth, but they just needed the facts to prove it.

I never personally asked the teachers to cheat. Either Reid or Ward separately identified teachers. I didn't know who all the teachers involved were until the case broke. I had some good and easy guesses but not much direct contact with the teachers. Reid and Ward were the teachers who would give them the instructions to cheat.

The method of cheating came from Reid and Ward as well. The three of us sat around the table, and they told me what they saw occur or had personally participated in at other schools in the Atlanta Public Schools system. In retrospect, they were also telling me strategies that were already going on at Parks before I started. Reid told me what happened at Harper-Archer Middle School. Somehow the teachers got copies of the test in advance. Then the teachers would teach to the test. If a question on the actual test was, "The refreshment committee needs 500 plastic cups for the dance. If cups are sold in packages of 200, how many packages need to be purchased?" The teachers would go over a question in class and use on the practice test a sample question such as "The booster club wants to buy 500 cupcakes for the dance. If cupcakes are sold in packages of 200, how many packages need to be purchased?"

Ward discussed what she saw at Beecher Hills Elementary School. There teachers made changes right in the classroom. They told the students and testing coordinators that they were cleaning up stray marks. What they were really doing was changing some of the answers for students who likely would not get the answer correct. All the teachers knew which students in their classes would need help (changes) on the test. Those were the test in which the most changes were made.

You knew there were some classrooms where no changes needed to be made; all of the students would have met the standard on their own. Those tests were not touched. That is part of the reason

2009 seems like it was intentional cheating to bring attention to Parks, Defense 3. The erasures made in 2009 were not necessary because the students began to excel and the amount of the changes were more than was needed. Classes and students who would have met the standard on their own had erasing on their tests that year. To put it in context, this is after the 2008 test irregularities were first found at Deerwood Elementary. That principal was ousted prior to administering the 2009 test. That was the test when I was completely checked out. I had direct communication with Reid and Ward in 2007. Less but continued communication to keep up the good work from the previous year in 2008. But in 2009, I had zero involvement. This is also why the term *orchestrated cheated* made sense to me. By 2009, one could argue it was a well-oiled machine that self-operated. I would argue it was a machine before I arrived and I continued to allow it to function. Principal Simms's team knew it and they knew if I was accused of cheating I would have a hard time defending it, so cheating excessively was a way to get me removed from Parks. Unfortunately for them, they didn't know the *Atlanta Journal–Constitution* was on the trail to expose us all.

The reality is I still participated enough, that whether it was the well-oiled machine or conspiracy, I acted. I made the decision with Reid and Ward to employ both methods of teaching to the test and changing answers. My most hands-on portion of the orchestration was to get Dr. Kiel, the testing coordinator, out of his office. Every testing day, I would take him for a nice long lunch, somewhere off campus like Pascal's or Busy Bee in the historic West End area. While he was out of the office, the teachers identified by Reid and Ward could get to work on changing answers. Luckily, testing day in a middle school is a good reason to let the kids let off a little steam by playing outside. Teachers not chosen by Reid and Ward to change answers were sent to monitor the students outside while the others were busy at work. There were some teachers who were completely clueless when the changes were being made. But several who should have been aware when the scores came back. They needed about two hours to get the changes made for all the students each year. I would call to let them know when we were completely gone and would give Ward a call to let them know when we were returning. Everything that needed to be done was completed by the small selected group of teachers. I learned in the criminal case the group grew each year. I surmise, that the teachers who couldn't ignore the significant score jumps knew what was going on and quickly identified the go-to people.

When I returned to the school with Dr. Kiel, the changes had been made, no irregularities were reported. I signed the form and off the test went. That is how I personally orchestrated cheating. Out of 180 days in a school year, I orchestrated actions on 10 days. It hurts me that very little discussion has been given to what we did the other 170 days when real teaching occurred.

Once I was able to evaluate my defense system and accept responsibility for my role, it allowed me to ask myself how I allowed myself to lie for so long. There was no one reason. Partly, I stuck to the script after people started making stuff up and changing stuff during the investigation. I became keenly concerned that there were so many untruths that were being said that it would have definitely been in the best interests of everybody, those above me and those below me, for me to stick to the script that had been said initially. If everyone stuck to the same script, it made it easier to remember and those who were exaggerating the truth in the investigation would eventually look like liars. And so, I did. I continued to stick to the script even with my attorneys who on several occasions asked for the whole story and nothing but the whole story. The Truth. Even when confronted with the inconsistencies in my defense theories, I stuck to the script. I continued to stick to the script because in my mind, in my heart, that was what was best for the people above me, that was what was best for me, and it was what was best for the people who worked below me, or with me, or at the school level. Some of my reasons were not for self-preservation; I truly cared about other people.

So, I stuck. I stayed there. I stayed there even though I had several opportunities to dodge the indictment, several opportunities to be left out of a lot of the stuff that had consequences. I stayed with the script because I didn't want to get anybody in trouble. I didn't want those above me to get in trouble and I didn't want the people below me to get in trouble for telling lies. I wasn't a snitch.

It didn't matter how much the child was taught or how much the child learned. If we didn't keep up with the targets, we would not be there to help the children continue the learning process. If we did not meet the AYP measurement, the school would close. The school that served the community would be no more. That was clear. So, I cheated for the kids and then I denied having any involvement in the scandal.

At some point, I realized that I needed to take some responsibility. Dodging the truth and sticking to the script were causing me to lose sleep. I was having anxiety attacks and dealing with depression issues. So, although I had come up with my defense mechanisms, these consequences made me take public responsibility for what happened at Parks Middle School under my watch.

I had already taken responsibility privately. I had taken responsibility prayerfully, but I needed to take some responsibility publicly to really be able to move past what had happened. A guilty plea was not only a guaranteed result, but it was the appropriate way to take responsibility publicly. Even if it had been worth the risk to go to trial and my legal defense was stronger based on the evidence the state did or didn't have, I now know I would have had to take the public responsibility to truly be free.

Dr. Hall gave us a clue that we should tell the whole truth. I felt it was her way of giving us permission to break from her script. She gave us permission prior to her last day at work when she sent out the video clip system-wide. The clip discussed the cheating that had taken place in APS. On her video, she appeared very surprised. She pretended she had just been enlightened to the unusual growth in test scores for the APS students. In hindsight, Dr. Hall was all about the scores and the data. She taught us how to read the data and evaluate it. She had experts showing the principals how to determine how many correct answers were needed at a school to ensure the standards were met year to year.

But in addition to pretending she was surprised, she also verbally articulated to "allow the chips to fall where they may." I wish that I had taken that statement more seriously then. I think now what she really was saying was save yourself. Tell whatever you have to tell or do whatever you have to do to protect yourself. Her video indicated to me whoever has to deal with the consequences would have to deal with the consequences either way. After the court proceedings began, her attorneys were very certain that the case would have to be dismissed because the evidence came from employees who were coerced by threatening their jobs. The attorneys argued the Garrity motion, which protects employees from incriminating themselves during an investigation. But the threat to cooperate with the investigation came from Dr. Hall herself. I believe, by this time, her legal team had advised her to put out that notice in hopes that the case against the teachers would go away and there would be no evidence against her. It would be easy for her to say let whoever deal with the consequences if she thought there would be none. The Garrity motion went to the Supreme Court of Georgia where it failed to overturn the case.

I missed that message at first glimpse, but I caught it the second time around, now that I'm looking in hindsight. She was releasing and washing her hands, pretty much saying she couldn't protect anybody. At that point, I believe she knew from the investigation that the jig was up and they had more than enough on all the players. Prior to then, I think Dr. Hall had worked relentlessly in not only trying to protect her reputation, but she knew that she had to protect everybody who was involved in cheating in an effort to protect that reputation. Like me, I think she thought as long as everyone stuck to the same script and sang the Blue Ribbon Commission song, we could all walk away unscathed.

I almost feel like even with the assignment to central office that we were put in those holding patterns in an effort to kind of keep our mouths shut, or to have our movements monitored. There would be times that I would even think the room I was in was bugged, that there was taping of everything that I said, so I just never knew. My paranoia continued throughout the trial preparation and all the way until I finally entered a plea agreement. I wasn't totally crazy; the Georgia Bureau of Investigation did have someone record a private conversation that led them nowhere. At the time of the recording, I was still sticking to the script.

So, once I decided to tell it, I told it all. That was the best decision that I probably made in the whole process. If I could be allowed the opportunity to do it again, I probably would have stood out earlier and told it earlier, and then allowed the chips to fall where they may.

Although this book discusses my openness and honesty on the stand and with the DA's office about what occurred in the APS cheating scandal, what is not included in this story is what occurred to me personally. This book does not address how this case affected my family, my future career, and my role as a minister. This book is not about that. Maybe in another writing I can openly discuss the personal side of this scandal, which was mentioned during my cross-examination. A defense attorney attempted to question me about the rumor of affairs that occurred during my time at Parks. These rumors had nothing to do with test scores, targets, or cheating. Rather, those matters have to do with the emotional toll working in APS took on my marriage and family for several years. The stress on the families of teachers and administrators is just one of the many not often discussed portions of this entire tragedy. Throughout my role as principal, my wife and I went through a series of separations both physically and emotionally that led to rumors, stories, and other issues. However, that is another story or another book.

Chapter 7

Dr. Hall Sets Targets

Dr. Hall passed away on March 2, 2015, while I was writing this book. I pray that she rests in peace. It is my hope that she agrees with me that she worked to provide a good education for the children of the Atlanta Public School system. Although there was cheating, I do not believe Dr. Hall's aim was to cheat the children of APS.

—Christopher Waller

In our US Constitution, we are all entitled to the presumption of innocence until proven guilty. Dr. Hall never received her presumption. In this case, that presumption went out the window with the first news report. Just like in my case, I did not feel our actions rose to the level of criminal action. Immoral, yes. Criminal, no. However, I had a chance to have a day in court. I had a chance to look at a prosecutor and jurors in the eye. Although I elected not to proceed to trial, I had the opportunity to "prove" my case if I chose to. Dr. Hall, at the time of this writing, has not had a chance to do so. Despite my descriptions of her to the DA's office and on the stand at trial, it is my belief that she is still innocent until proven guilty at trial. That is the difference between a moral wrong and a legal wrong. It is important to me that despite what people say or think about Dr. Hall, that this message is made clear. Like myself and the others accused, Dr. Hall worked hard for her accomplishments before and while she was the superintendent of the Atlanta Public Schools. A few bad years should not erase the background that made up Dr. Beverly Hall.

Dr. Beverly Hall was born in Montego Bay, Jamaica, and moved to the United States for college. After receiving her undergraduate degree from Brooklyn College in 1970, she furthered her education by later receiving both a master's degree from CUNY and an EdD from Fordham University in 1990.

Dr. Hall taught English in a public junior high school in Brooklyn, New York, and began her career in school administration first as a junior high coordinator then as principal of two junior high schools. In 1994, she became superintendent of Community School District No. 27 in Queens, New York, and was then appointed as chief executive for instructional and student support services in the New York City public school system. From 1995 to 1999, she served as superintendent of the Newark Public Schools in Newark, New Jersey.

In 1999, Dr. Hall was appointed superintendent of the Atlanta Public Schools until her retirement during the scandal. In 2009, she was named National Superintendent of the Year by the American Association of School Administrators. A portion of Dr. Hall's award was due to the gains in the student scores during her tenure.

In 2011, a four-hundred-page report compiled by more than one hundred professionals was submitted to the governor of Georgia. This document, referred to as the Governor's Office of Student Achievement report, or the "GOSA" report, was an "overview of the evidence and our findings." The findings of the specially appointed investigators were that "cheating occurred throughout [Atlanta Public] school district." The investigators went on to say, "Our investigation found organized and systemic wrongdoing in APS well before the administration of the 2009 CRCT." The report detailed many of their findings, specifically how "targets" worked.

It was the targets that caused the excessive pressure to cheat. The targets that were higher than what the federal government required under AYP. Although the threat of closure under AYP was a concern for Parks, the higher standard of targets was a looming issue to be resolved.

The idea behind targets was that if one group of kids did well in fifth grade, for example, the next year, the next group of fifth-grade kids should be able to outperform the group before them. The targets didn't follow the children to see if they were really growing. In layman's terms, if a child entered fifth grade scoring 60 percent, and the previous fifth-grade class before him scored 68 percent. That new fifth grader, with the lower scoring ability was expected to outperform the 68 percent testers. Schools didn't get credit under the targets for bringing that fifth grader who was at 60 percent up to 65 or 66 percent because they still did not outperform the previous students.

If targets were done correctly, it would have followed the child. Following the student would have looked at a class that scored 60 percent and set the goal for the next year at 63 percent. A 3 percent increase would have been reasonable based on the class. Taking a class already behind and expecting them to improve twice as fast as the classes that were ahead of them just doesn't make sense.

Targets didn't do that. Targets said if these set of teachers scored X, regardless of who they get next year, and regardless of how far behind the kids are next year, they should be able to move those children three percentage points further than the children they moved last year. It didn't matter if in the previous year all the students were geniuses. That's how the targets failed, with unrealistic and unattainable goals.

The GOSA report stated:

The unreasonable pressure to meet annual "targets" was the primary motivation for teachers and administrators to cheat on the CRCT in 2009 and previous years. Virtually every teacher who confessed to cheating spoke of the inordinate stress the district placed on meeting targets and the dire consequences for failure. Dr. Hall articulated it as: "No exceptions. No excuses." If principals did not meet targets within three years, she declared, they will be replaced and "I will find someone who will meet targets." Dr. Hall replaced 90% of the principals during her tenure. Principals told teachers that failure to improve CRCT scores would result in negative evaluations or job termination. The unambiguous message was to meet targets by any means necessary.

We do not express any opinion as to the merits of targets. However, targets were implemented by APS in such a way that teachers and administrators believed that they had to choose between cheating to meet targets or failing to meet targets and losing their jobs.

When Dr. Beverly Hall became superintendent in 1999, she implemented many new programs and education strategies. Dr. Hall managed the district by relying heavily upon data, as opposed to being a hands-on leader. In this regard, she implemented the "target" program, which held teachers and principals responsible for student achievement. These targets were used to quantify expectations so that academic progress was measurable, based primarily on the prior years' CRCT results.

The major difference between APS targets and AYP standards is that under the target system, a school is not only required to move students from the bottom to the middle (i.e., from the "not meets" standards to the "meets" standards category on the CRCT), but schools are also required to move students from the middle to the top (i.e., from "meets" standards to "exceeds" standards). In this way, a school must focus on improving achievement for both lower performing and higher performing students.

Targets are set annually by the APS administration and approved by the Board of Education. The administration, with assistance from an outside consultant, sets these targets for the district, every school and each grade. The administration notifies the schools of their targets in terms of percentage. For example, one target at a school might be to increase the percentage of students "exceeding" standards in math by 3%, while at the same time reducing the number of students "not meeting" math standards by 2%. This allows each teacher in every classroom to know exactly how many students must "meet" or "exceed" the target objective.

Low-performing schools are required to improve by a greater margin each year than higher-performing schools. Thus, a higher burden is placed upon the lower-performing schools.

As schools achieve their targets, the next year, the targets increase. For example, if 50% of last year's fourth grade students met expectations in math on the CRCT, then this year that target might increase to 63%. Targets are set based upon the previous years' group of students. According to teachers and administrators, this element of targets, combined with the fact that the targets increase every year, makes them unreasonable. For instance, if last year's fourth graders were mostly high-performing students, but the fourth-grade class this year contains more low performers, the fourth-grade targets are still set based on last year's high performing students' scores. Teachers and administrators we interviewed consistently referred to this as "comparing apples to oranges" rather than "apples to apples."

Schools that meet 70% of their targets receive bonuses for every employee from bus drivers to the principal. These bonuses range from $50 to $2000 per person, depending on what the percentage of the targets the school as a whole achieves. Dr. Hall stood to get financial gain based on whether the district met targets. Over the years, she received tens of thousands of dollars based on the reported CRCT results.

Schools that meet targets will "make the floor" at Convocation, the district's annual, system-wide celebration held at the Georgia Dome to recognize schools that make targets and improve CRCT scores. Attendance by all faculty and administrators is mandatory. Faculty at schools that hit targets sit "on the floor." Those that do not make targets are relegated to sit in the uppermost sections of the Dome. Throughout this investigation, it became clear that for many in the district, especially principals, it was extremely important to "make the floor."

On the other hand, if a school fails to meet targets, its principal and teachers are likely to be placed on a professional development plan (PDP) and receive negative performance evaluations. Some are terminated.

Student achievement comprises 25% of principals' evaluations, the single heaviest weighted item. Dr. Hall made it clear that if within three years a school does not meet targets, then she will replace the principal with someone who will. Principals put the same pressure on teachers to meet targets by placing teachers on PDPs, publicly humiliating them, or threatening termination. The PDP is supposed to be a tool for helping teachers and principals improve areas of weakness. Instead, the PDP became a weapon to punish and threaten teachers for having low test scores. The message heard by teachers and principals was that the only way out of the PDP was to increase test scores. . . .

When principals, in groups of 10 to 12, met annually with Dr. Hall, each school's scores were displayed on large colorful graphs framed and hung on the wall around her conference room. During the meeting, Dr. Hall would ask each principal, one by one, "are you going to meet targets this year?" No one dared tell her "no."

. . . The monetary bonus for meeting targets provided little incentive to cheat. But fear of termination and public ridicule in faculty and principals' meetings drove numerous educators to cross ethical lines. Further, because targets rose annually, teachers found it increasingly difficult to achieve them. After a few years of increases, teachers found the targets unattainable and resorted to cheating. Multiple years of test misconduct in the district compounded the level of cheating that was required annually to not only match the prior year's false scores but also to surpass them. The gap between where the students were academically and the targets they were trying to reach grew larger.

The cumulative effect of cheating over a decade on the CRCT made meeting targets more difficult with each passing year. To maintain the gains of the past years while achieving the target of the current year required more cheating than in prior years. Once cheating started it became a house of cards that collapsed upon itself. . . .

Pressure to meet targets and improve student's CRCT scores was the single, most frequent explanation given by teachers for why they cheated. Most teachers, and many principals, described an oppressive environment at APS where the entire focus of the district had become achieving test *scores rather than teaching children. Incremental, yearly progress by students was not enough unless the school met targets. Individual student progress was not as important as the school, as a whole, increasing its overall CRCT scores. In the end, meeting targets became more about the adults than the children.*

One thing not mentioned by the special investigators findings on "targets" were the "cut scores." Dr. Hall brought in statisticians to explain to the small groups of principals what number of correct answers were needed to reach each school's targets. This information was never presented as "use this number to determine how many answers to change." However, there was no other relevant or valid use of this information.

In the Casey Foundation article "Beating the Odds at Parks Middle School," the unsaid guidance was written so eloquently. "Hunley helped Parks's teachers to look at the data and to understand what was required to meet Adequate Yearly Progress and why they were not achieving it. 'We had some very intelligent teachers who just didn't understand the process,' she explains." The process was how to use the CRCT previous scores to know what answers need to be changed.

The article goes on to quote Hunley: "Once we got the numbers right, we could put names with the numbers. . . . We were able to pull the data by teachers, so we knew who was being effective and who was not. When we identified the effective teachers, we could look more closely at they were doing." Stated in real talk, we use the numbers to find out which teachers could achieve the scores on their own and which teacher's students would need artificial help.

Chapter 8

Good Friday? Racketeer Influenced and Corrupt Organizations (RICO) Act

On Good Friday, the district attorney of Fulton County indicted thirty-eight educators who worked in the Atlanta Public School system. The DA's office accused them of test tampering, pressuring people to cheat, cheating, or for willfully turning a blind eye to the cheating. The same day Jesus was crucified, the day Jesus was hung on the cross to die for the sins of the world, was the same day the district attorney indicted thirty-eight educators in the city of Atlanta.

When I got news of the indictment, my heart dropped. There had been a lot of rumors and media coverage that it was coming. I called my lawyers when I saw Damany Lewis on the news walking out of the grand jury room. The story was about the number of witnesses testifying before the grand jury in this case. Until the actual indictment occurred, I thought it could all still go away. I know I was not the only educator who felt that way. In Atlanta, the fire department had had a cheating scandal when they were cheating on supervisors' tests. The police department had had scandals where officers were falsifying documents. The Fulton County DA's office had not indicted them, so I just knew that this indictment would never come.

But I will never forget, Good Friday, when the grand jury handed out the indictments, almost four years after the investigation began. I had to prepare for the Good Friday service and my message to preach to God's people. Good Friday is the day that Christians commemorate the crucifixion of their Lord and their Savior, Jesus Christ, and the text that I raised for that message was "Father, forgive them, for they know not what they do." I preached from the topic "What's Good about Good Friday?"

In the Bible, bad things happened on Good Friday: Jesus was crucified, beaten, spat upon, humiliated, a crown of thorns were put upon his head, he was hung out to die, and he was pierced by a Roman soldier in the side. Nothing good really happened on what we call Good Friday. But on that day, Jesus called for us to be forgiven. He said, "Father, forgive them, they know not what they do." Despite all of the bad that happened on Good Friday, because of forgiveness, Good Friday may not have been as bad as it could have been.

When I read the indictment on that Good Friday, which was posted online on the *Atlanta Journal–Constitution*'s website, I found out that I had been indicted under the Racketeer Influenced and Corrupt Organizations (RICO) Act. I didn't even know what racketeering was, but I knew it was something major. My assumption about racketeering charges was that it was for Mafia-style, drug-dealing style businesses and major drug dealing organizations. I could not have imagined that an educator could have been indicted for racketeering.

I remember reading the indictment, going through it line by line, and saying to myself how inappropriate and inadequate it was. It appeared to be in short reaching. Of course, at this time I was still on the same script. Despite a large number of people being involved district-wide, the indictment targeted only thirty-eight people.

I was charged with racketeering, several counts of false statements, and theft by taking. I resented the theft charge. I was not a thief and I had not taken anything. I had given to the students, to the families, and to the community. I had paid their utility bills, rent money, and helped with HIV medicine out of my own pocket. My defense mechanisms went up. It made it easy for me to skip right past the things in the indictment that were correct and focus on the fact that I hadn't taken anything. I sent kids on trips all over the world. I had not taken from them. I had spent my time serving and giving from the heart.

Yes, I would now be held accountable for my part in the overall operation of cheating, but racketeering was something I had not participated in. However, I was indicted, along with others. What I learned is that no matter what specific evidence they had on me, I could be lumped in with the organization if they could make it appear that I played even a small part. My legal team had heard that a RICO indictment was possible, but until the actual indictment was complete, one could never know who would be charged and how.

As I mentioned, I was not honest with my team initially. I recited from the script that I had used throughout the investigation. As each side dug into their positions and their view of the scandal, I stuck closer to mine. The media had an angle of selling the story; they highlighted lies because it sold papers and got people to their websites. Some teachers dug in to their untruths that helped them keep their immunity. The prosecutors dug in because they had invested too much and had too many eyes watching. In hindsight, I wished like hell that I had been very forthcoming from day one with the attorneys. As they helped me understand the process, I think if I had been more honest with my attorneys initially, I could have helped them navigate the process in my defense much, much better. The DA offered opportunities for me to come and talk even before the indictment. But I didn't take advantage of that opportunity nor was I pushed by my counsel because the story they had at the time of the opportunity was that I knew nothing and did nothing and everyone was lying. I had the opportunity to avoid any indictment that would come.

I didn't take the opportunity to not be indicted because I didn't just want a good outcome, I wanted a perfect outcome. In light of this case, it may be hard for people to picture me as selfless, but I wanted everybody to be cleared. I wasn't interested in just me getting out of it when I knew that I had done some things, even if I had not acknowledged it to anyone yet. I knew I had allowed and even ordered some things to happen under my watch, so it wasn't about getting out of it. I was only willing to get out of it and not have any consequences, if everybody was able to get out of it and not have any consequences. Since I did not speak up soon enough, the case had been indicted, and now I was labeled as a racketeer.

It was almost like I was in a cult and I operated from a team, cult, group perspective while everybody else was pretty much operating from an individual perspective. The moment Dr. Hall changed her story and started discussing falling chips, I realized this had become every man for himself, and God forgive us all. Even after I decided to throw in the towel, I wanted to give everybody connected to my scandal a chance to speak for themselves. I rather they chose to take a plea because that was best for them and their family and not because I made it necessary by telling the truth first. I didn't try to go out and be the hero. I tried to lay low and allow the process to go forward. While I was allowing the process to move forward, I was still thinking in my mind that it was going to go away and that the judge would dismiss the case. When that didn't work, I began to hang on the Garrity motion as a way to make this nightmare end. My lawyers believed the court would agree that the teachers' rights had been violated when we were mandated to talk to investigators whether we wanted to or not. I thought all of that would come into play at some point, and so I held the line.

I could not believe that District Attorney Howard indicted the case under the RICO Act because I had always in my life looked up to him. Whether I liked his decisions on cases or not, I still had a great amount of respect for him. Inasmuch as I understood him to be a fair man, when he indicted educators as racketeers, I knew then that the possibility of me working with DA Howard was limited. I felt that the he did not see us as human beings trying to do good things in a difficult situation, but rather he saw us as gangsters and mobsters. I began to lose respect for a man that I had looked up to, the man who had helped my family with a major case after my goddaughter's death. I may have been able to accept criminal misdemeanor charges under the circumstances, but I really couldn't grasp the fact that DA Howard, whom I had respected, saw educators as racketeers.

Chapter 9

Testalying

The Atlanta Public Schools trial began on September 29, 2014. It was expected to last three to six months. There were hundreds of witnesses. All I knew was I had to wait for the DA's office to call me to come to court. I was a topic from the beginning of the case. I knew I was considered the "poster child" for cheating by the media, to the public, and to the DA's office. The news coverage of the scandal had begun in 2009, and it did not let up throughout the five years up to the trial. By day four of the trial, it appeared from the media that all of the testimony was about Parks Middle and Christopher Waller. I had already entered my plea agreement several months earlier, so I didn't go to court, but I did see the news stories. I had a front-row seat to the cheating culture of APS, but I had the same view of the trial as the rest of the public. On day four, I and the rest of the world saw clips of Stacey Webb Johnson testifying at the trial on the eleven o'clock evening news. But I did not agree with her version of the facts.

I became furious. I called LaDawn at eight o'clock the next morning.

Chris: What is going on?!? Are they trying to make me look bad?

LaDawn: I saw the story, too. I was going to call you from the car this morning.

Chris: That is not how that stuff happened. Stacy Webb Johnson did not resign because of anonymous letters. This is the first time I ever even heard that. I don't understand why Clint and Fani chose to walk down that road of allowing these people to further damage my credibility when they're going to put me on the stand after them. After they've demeaned me, I have to get on the stand and contradict their witnesses. Are they setting me up?

LaDawn: They may not even get into the stuff you are concerned about during the trial. And if they do, all you can do is tell the truth. Let them worry about cleaning up the contradictions. Witnesses contradict each other all the time. I don't think it's a setup, they told you after the plea you are no longer a defendant.

Chris: Can I bring this stuff up in court on my own?

LaDawn: You need to focus on answering the questions they ask. Your one job is to tell the truth and get off the stand, so you are done with this chapter of your life. But if the State or one of the defense attorneys brings it up, go for your record. Today, just go from the heart. Put all that stuff in your book.

I considered what LaDawn told me. I had concerns that people would think I was taking advantage of my involvement. That was not the reason I chose to write my story. I wanted people to hear the parts of the story that did not come out in the testimony, during the investigation or in the media. I was already the poster child for the cheating scandal. I was already under scrutiny. I felt that a final repentance for my actions was to again put myself in the line of fire so that I could be sure another side of the story is in the public domain. I can't speak to what happened in the rest of APS, but I know what happened at Parks Middle School.

Throughout my time at Parks, I talked about a team concept and a team approach. But I was truly talking about working as a team for teaching and teamwork for instruction. When Dr. Hall talked about building a team she was talking about picking people you could trust to help you get the scores up by any means necessary. As she said, "There were no excuses." Throughout the case, the teachers and investigators tried to make it appear that when I told my staff to "get on the bus," I meant join my select team of cheating teachers. But "get on the bus" wasn't my attempt to get the whole school on board for erasing and cheating. I was trying to get the whole school on board for teaching the children and differentiating instruction. I maintain I did not induce teachers to erase test personally, not even by innuendo. I believe in the team approach. One of the many reasons I continued to stick to my story as it was falling apart was the team. I did not want to hurt anyone who was a part of my team, superiors and subordinates.

The DA put Stacey Webb Johnson (who was known as Stacey Webb back then) on the witness stand. Her testimony did not match the way I remembered the facts. She did not resign because of cheating allegations.

Webb was a math facilitator when I arrived. The last principal, Michael Simms, hired her. There was an incident involving Webb and Mrs. Simms, the principal's wife, at school. Relationships between staff members was a part of the APS culture. The conflicts of interest created through these personal relationships complicated the scandal. Loyalty to subordinates or colleagues is one thing. Personal relationships create a higher level of loyalty.

As math facilitator at Parks, Webb supervised all the math teachers. My understanding was that she did not even have a teaching certificate nor had ever taught a class before. It's hard to teach teachers how to teach if you've never taught yourself. You can't teach what you don't know. I believe she wanted to be promoted because she asked me to get rid of Dr. Kiel when I became principal. Before Simms was fired, he was in the process of getting rid of Dr. Kiel. Simms was in the process of promoting his team. My perspective makes me believe Principal Simms's team included Stacey Webb and Fabiola Aurelien.

Prior to me coming to the school, the teachers did not have the data from the previous CRCT. While Simms was the principal, I came to learn that Webb was one of few staff members who had the school's test data. Teachers knew the previous tests scores were low, but they didn't know which students in which classrooms contributed to the low scores, or which students passed and what their scores were—except Webb.

When I became principal, it was obvious Webb was not cutting it as the math facilitator. If I was going to turn that school around, I needed good math instruction. It didn't help that she continued to be very insubordinate. While Simms was principal, Webb came to work late. I'm not talking about ten or fifteen minutes late. I'm talking about school starts at 7:30 a.m. and she shows up at 10:00 a.m. And when I became principal, she continued along the same vein. She arrived whenever she wanted to and left when she wanted to. She came to work dressed in a way that I considered highly inappropriate. The church ladies would say she was only "half-dressed." As a principal, I did not approve.

Cheryl Hunley, the state facilitator, attended Parks every day because Parks did not meet AYP and was on the Needs Improvement 8 list. A Title I school that fails to make AYP as defined by the state for two consecutive years is designated "in need of improvement, Year 1" and receives specific consequences. For each subsequent year that a school fails to meet its AYP goals, the school's "in need of improvement" status advances and the school faces additional consequences. A school is no longer considered "in need of improvement" when it meets AYP for two consecutive years.

Hunley, among others, made several comments and notations about the attitude and the attire of Stacey Webb. She documented Webb's insubordination, her nonresponsiveness, and noncompliance with the state facilitator. It was obvious we had to let Webb go. In APS, the facilitator positions are annual positions that are renewed every year. When Michael Pitts learned I was firing Webb, he immediately decided that he would hire her. I found that very strange.

I couldn't understand why a supervisor would hire a person who didn't fit the bill for one of his subordinates. Particularly when he knows she is being fired for incompetence and insubordination. It wasn't until she changed positions that news about her not having a teaching certificate was relayed to me. I did not think she could fill her new position without having a teaching certificate.

Pitts attempted to hire her anyway, until Monique Ross from the APS personnel department said that she could not process the paperwork to hire a math facilitator who had not met the minimum requirements. The requirements included teaching for at least three years, serve in a leadership capacity for at least two years, and be certified. Pitts pushed Ross to do it anyway. When she refused, she was the next person to resign. Ross got married and moved to Barbados, but she never processed the application for Stacey Webb. When Webb couldn't qualify to be the math facilitator, she resigned. I think she resigned to go back to school to the complete the classes needed for a teaching certificate.

On the stand, Stacey Webb Johnson said she was forced to resign because she wrote anonymous letters about me. The very first time I learned that she ever wrote an anonymous letter was when I read the article in the newspaper the day after her testimony. I didn't know about any anonymous letters until I read it during the trial, I could not force her to resign about something I never knew about.

Until her testimony on the stand, I thought she resigned because she could not get the job she wanted in Pitts's office. When Simms was the principal, Webb had been paid extra to work the after-school program, 21st Century, a grant program that would be rewritten by the Casey Foundation. That position required her to stay late at times. She was always paid to stay late, despite the fact she did not show up to work on time. When I became principal, she didn't even try to be punctual.

I strongly disagree with Webb's testimony about being harassed and intimidated by me. She described it as being escorted out the building by the police. An officer did walk with her to the car. But he was just standing there at the time, and she was a woman who needed her personal belongings carried. It wasn't a punitive thing and it wasn't an escort. When she resigned, Pitts had asked her to come to the SRT 2 office. Stacey had lots of heavy stuff to carry and I asked the officer simply because he was in the vicinity and did not mind. If I wanted her forcibly escorted out of the building, I would have gone down with them to walk her out and make sure she was out. Then I would have made sure there was formal documentation of her being escorted out of the building for my own protection.

I hate that something I did to be a gentleman was turned into escorting her out of the building because she reported cheating. That is one of my biggest complaints about this case. There was cheating at Parks, but this case has turned the best-intentioned statements, comments, and actions into a part of this racketeering theory. The little things help to make the conspiracy so much bigger that it completely overshadows the good that occurred at my school. After she left Parks, Webb got married and added Johnson to her last name. Her testimony on the stand, for reasons I may never know, did not match up with my memory of the facts.

On the stand, Fabiola Aurelien, a math teacher at Parks, talked about kids not being able to read in high school because of what happened at the middle school. Students are supposed to learn how to read while they are in elementary school. They came to Parks not able to read. The reading problem of the high school students started well before they got to us.

It is important again to note that Aurelien knew that there was education going on along with the cheating, because she was one of the teachers who really taught. In fact, she was one of the best math teachers we've had come through that building. She taught kids every single day. She was a hard worker and didn't sit down at all during the work day. To say nothing was going on in the middle school was a lie.

Aurelien saw the instruction; she even helped other teachers with the instruction. She knew that teaching took place, but when she testified, she pretended that the school was a pull-the-rabbit-out-of-the-hat school. That's so far from what Parks Middle School was. At Parks, the teachers worked hard for the most part every single day. There were pockets of students that caused us concern. Those students were the ones we couldn't catch up quick enough, no matter how well we taught. No matter how hard we tried, we just couldn't help them keep up with the moving targets.

The targets were set such that they continued to increase. Schools were not only trying to meet a basic level of success, they were also required to show improvements each year. So even with the best instruction, we could improve the students' scores but not enough to meet the consistently rising targets.

Parks Assistant Principal Merita Brown testified on the stand that she reported a kid was using a textbook to cheat on the test. She testified that reports of cheating like that one went ignored. That's the furthest thing from the truth. First of all, it would be difficult for a student to be able to use a textbook to assist them on the CRCT, because the CRCT does not test material necessarily found in a textbook. The CRCT measures if students have mastered the standards or the objectives of the common core. A textbook would not have helped any student cheat on the test. Furthermore, Brown was experienced enough to know that reports of that type first went to the testing coordinator and put in writing.

Brown had been the interim principal prior to my arrival. She had thirty-plus years' experience in education and had worked in APS for quite some time. If what she said had happened, she would not have reported that to me per APS policy. The policy states the principal is not in charge of testing or the first report. Dr. Alfred Keil, the testing coordinator, would have reported it to me if Brown did make a report of that nature. I never recall her reporting anything to me about a kid using a textbook to cheat on the CRCT. Never, ever, have I heard of anybody, talking about any kid using a textbook during the test. That is something so unusual I would have remembered if it happened. In light of what I have admitted to, there is no reason for me to lie about this.

This is just another example of the witch hunt. Although none of these stories were exposed during the Blue Ribbon Commission report, after teachers were promised immunity to testify, stories like this appeared. You may be asking yourself, why would one lie about something like this? Remember, all the investigations in this case were not aimed at just proving that the tests were changed by human intervention. That was determined when the first analysis was done by CTB/McGraw-Hill. The investigation was to determine if there was "system-wide and organized" cheating. The investigators presumed everyone was involved until they proved they were not. If someone pointed the finger at another teacher, that teacher was now on the hook to help connect the dots to prove the investigator's theory. I believe witnesses like Assistant Principal Brown felt the need to make some connection to show they were not involved by telling the investigators she reported cheating rather than assisted with it. A small white lie to protect one's teaching certificate and way of life was probably worth it. I can assure you that Brown did not report that to me.

When I met Brown the first time and introduced myself with "I'm Chris Waller," she shook my hand and replied, "I'm retiring." At the end of that school year, she did retire. I do not know if she was on Principal Simms's team before I arrived, but she certainly did not want to be there after he left. I didn't have a dog in the fight with testing in 2005. I wouldn't be held responsible for the scores that year, and I was too busy still trying to find out where the front door was. I came in that year and all I did was work on discipline. I started trying to build the team sentiment and trying to get a culture in place where teachers could teach and children could learn. I had not moved, orchestrated, or been a part of any cheating that may have occurred in 2005. So, if a kid was using a book and it was reported to me by anyone, I would have followed protocol. Unlike later, I had nothing to hide. I wasn't worried about any red flags bringing attention to the test because I had not done anything wrong at that time.

When I arrived at Parks in 2005, all of the students had scored in the 295–298 range during the CRCT in 2004. They were right on the cusp of passing the test. I remember looking at that data with the state's school facilitator, Cheryl Hunley, and commenting to her, "This won't be that hard." Most of the students were just one question away from the score we needed to pull Parks from the brink of closure. It did not click then, but the probability of that number of students all being only one question short of passing is probably as likely as the erasure stats. However, no one had analyzed that result on those tests or that probability, but I now suspect human intervention had to be involved in those scores as well. Stacey Webb was the only one with the scores before I arrived. I would not be surprised if she did the math wrong and didn't have enough questions changed the year before I came. Lisa Coston summed it up the best in her article "Report Eviscerates Atlanta Schools for Decade of Systematic Cheating":

The investigators hired Professor of Educational Measurement and Evaluation Gregory Cizek, from the University of North Carolina, to review the erasure analysis. He concluded that the probability that the high WTR erasures occurred randomly was like having Atlanta's sports venue The Georgia Dome filled to capacity, with "every person in the Dome being seven feet tall."

"Amazingly, many APS teachers had high WTR erasures in all three subject areas — English/language arts, reading and math," the report states.

"Not only did numerous teachers do something that was virtually impossible one time, but did it three times in a row. Even more amazing, several teachers in the same school did this multiple times."

Cheryl Hunley is quoted several times in the Casey Foundation article "Beating the Odds at Parks Middle School." A part of Dr. Hall's promotion of Parks included a multi-page article on the gains of the school's scores. The statements in the article by many of the people who testified against Parks and what they said on the stand are in direct contradiction. The GOSA report refers to the article in their findings to show that Hall must have known about cheating. The investigators cite the failure of APS to continue to investigate after the improbable scores. They considered that Hall's "publicly touting" Parks.

The entire Casey Foundation article "Beating the Odds at Parks Middle School" is included in the GOSA report. However, some of the highlights of the article, in retrospect, highlight the confidence in which the cheating was "touted." The article made statements such as "An inner-city middle school with many risk factors—94 percent of its students are poor—has experienced a dramatic turnaround during the past few years. Why has this happened?" The article goes on to take quotes from teachers and staff that support the notion that the turnaround was caused by "support, relentless focus on data, and involvement by a broad range of partners and community residents."

The article describes Parks's eight-year run as a "Needs Improvement" school but lets readers know that the eighth graders rose their ability to exceed state standards. Large text that stands out from the article says, "In one year the percentage of eighth graders meeting standards in reading increased by 43 percentage points, from 35% to 78%." The article shows a photo of Elizabeth Kelly, a Casey Foundation education consultant, going over the data on test scores displayed prominently in the school's hallway.

The article is honest in that it states it was written by Atlanta Civic Site Diarist Sarah Tonan. The article also mentions that Parks is located in the Pittsburgh neighborhood of Atlanta. The article states, "Pittsburgh has been a focus of the work of the Annie E. Casey Foundation's Atlanta 'Civic Site,' a long-term effort to make low-income neighborhoods more supportive of children and their families." Said another way, this article was written by the donors to show off the good work their foundation had accomplished by supporting the neighborhood school.

Not mentioned during the investigation of the case but found through Tonan's interviews and review of the scores, "Waller was not the first principal to improve test scores at Parks. During the previous three years, test scores had increased steadily, the result of a new approach to leadership begun by Superintendent Hall's 'School Reform Team 2' . . . according to SRT 2 Executive Director Michael Pitts." Subtly captured in the article is a sincere belief that cheating was occurring before I became principal at Parks.

The article also caught another factor that was not often highlighted during the investigation. The previous principal as the article correctly lays out ". . . the principal who helped achieve this success had been dismissed in the summer of 2004, the result of alleged misconduct at a different school. This principal's dismissal caused unrest among the faculty and the community, and the test scores faltered, creating an extra challenge for Waller."

This challenge never went away. As much as there were administrative changes throughout the school, the previous principal's "team" who help raised those scores did not like the changes I made. I cannot say enough times that I believe the extreme change in numbers was an attempt to get rid of me by that former team. Cheryl Hunley was in the school to help with the transition. The article summarized Hunley's report in a way that supports my beliefs.

> *"Many of the teachers talked about how well the students had done before [Mr. Waller was hired]," Hunley remembers, ". . . They perceived that the years before were so much better. They did not understand that the data did not substantiate what they were saying."*
>
> *She began to realize that their evaluation of the school's performance was based not on student achievement, but on how comfortable they were in their job. . . . "One of the things Mr. Waller had to do was break up that comfort zone because that was not good for the kids. They equated doing well with doing what they wanted to do."*

The reason I know that cheating occurred is because some of my teachers were very smart people: smart enough to understand the concepts of data and test scores, smart enough to organize the way to cheat on their own without my personal direction, and certainly smart enough to work on a process to get rid of me by excessive cheating.

When asked during the Casey Foundation's article, "Beating the Odds at Parks Middle School," Damany Lewis excitedly reported the GED course, Saturday School, and the six-week computer class that helped parents get a free computer was the cause for success. He wasn't forced to make these statements; it was completely his choice. Yet when he was interviewed during the multiple investigations, he suddenly remembers being asked to get into something undetected. We remember this encounter completely different. Part of my involvement included keeping "plausible deniability." I didn't discuss cheating directly with the teachers. Yet according to Lewis, the question about getting into something undetected was a direct order by me to open the booklets, copy it for each grade, resealing the packages with a lighter, and placing the copies in the cars of two other co-conspirators. The reality is, this was all organized by Lewis himself. He was smart enough to make that happen, just as he was smart enough to make a good showing for the Casey Foundation article. All that makes me theorize he is smart enough to orchestrate an over-cheating scheme to get rid of me.

Chapter 10

Apples and Oranges

I grew up in a rural town outside of Macon, Georgia. My home town of Sofkee, Georgia, will only show up on very few maps. It sits between Macon and Warner Robins on Highway 247 in the middle of the state. My mother's side of the family lived in a rural section of town where there were limited activities that we could do. We did not have all of the video games and computers that children have today. We had to create and make our own fun.

One of the things that we would often do for fun is play school. I was the oldest, and when we played, I would always be the teacher. When we played church, I was also the preacher. So as a kid, I always had a desire to teach the little bit that I knew.

Once I finished high school and went on to college, I recognized that science was a subject that wasn't well embraced by children. I reflected upon my academic career and I can only remember one science teacher, Ms. Reid, who taught me chemistry in high school. She really made a difference for me and helped me grasp the basic principles of science. She made me fall in love with science.

I attended Paine College in Augusta for my undergraduate degree, where I studied science. I wanted to try medical school, but the labs became overwhelming to me. After the first lab course in college,

I changed my mind. I am not fond of blood or certain smells. I knew medicine was not for me, so I decided to major in education.

While I was in college, my mother, who was a teacher, would take me as an additional chaperone for her school trips. While still a student, I had a chance to see public education at work while trying to decide on my major and future career. My mother always taught in some of the worst or the lowest socioeconomic areas in the city. I watched her expose children to new opportunities through the field trips I chaperoned. I followed, what I later learned was a destined passion, in my mother's footsteps as a schoolteacher.

I landed my first job after doing several internships in the Augusta area. I did my student teaching at Tubman Middle School, under Debbie Alexander, a seventh-grade teacher, who is now a principal at a school in Augusta. Tubman is a low-income, Title I school in Richmond County, Georgia. It is a military county, for which Augusta is the county seat, with one of the largest military bases in Georgia, Fort Gordon. The military base and many of the military families lived in the rural area of the county. Tubman Middle was located in Augusta, only four miles from the Medical College of Georgia, two miles from Augusta State University, and a mile from Paine College.

Paine College was one of the few colleges in the state at the time that would not allow you to student teach unless you had passed a Praxis. A Praxis is a test that measures would-be teachers' knowledge and skills. The tests are taken by future teachers as part of the certification process. That meant that once you graduated from college you were already prepared for certification. I graduated from Paine in 1996.

Tubman Middle was in a very old and historical building in the middle of several housing projects where gangs were becoming popular. Students defined themselves based on where they lived. We had several situations where rivalry projects' communities would bring some issues left over from the weekend into the school.

As a student teacher, I taught seventh-grade math and science. It was then I took the first weapon from a student. TJ was upset because a boy said something to his sister, who was in the seventh grade as well. I just happened to be standing there when TJ was going to approach the other young man with the weapon. I grabbed him and just held him. Ronnie Harrison, the principal, showed up and just told me to keep holding him. I'll never forget that. He didn't offer any assistance. He just told me to keep holding him until the resource officer could get there. This was the first of many experiences.

But at the end of the year, after successful completion of my student teaching, I was offered a job at Tubman. The principal was moving on to another school, but he thought well enough of me to send me to interview with the future principal. Dr. Hawthorne Welter offered me my first real job as a teacher.

I would be an eighth-grade science teacher at Tubman, which meant that I would teach lots of the kids with whom I had worked as a student teacher the previous year. Although my major was education with an emphasis in science and physical education, my adviser at the college, Dr. Yvonne Shaw, made it clear that there would be absolutely no way in the world that I would ever teach physical education. She said it and she meant it. So, she set my student teaching up for math and science. Subsequently, I was only offered jobs in science. I never have had an opportunity to be offered a teaching position in math. I'm thankful for that, because I've had an excellent opportunity to really change the outlook of many people and the way they look at the science curriculum.

But I taught eighth-grade science on a team as its youngest member. In fact, I was the youngest teacher in the building. Because I was right out of college, kids felt I understood them. If things went wrong in another class, they came to me because the older teachers didn't understand. Age likely was not the only problem, either. That year, I remember the community issue was the transportation district lines. The transportation lines were set up to send the lowest income communities to Tubman. The students and teachers couldn't connect because of age and the difference in socioeconomics.

I taught on a team of teachers, each with a different subject. Ms. Calloway, Ms. Fortunay, and Mr. Kicklighter worked as a team. Ms. Fortunay, the math teacher, retired from South Carolina and drove over the state line to Georgia to teach. Ms. Calloway taught English for twenty-nine years, and Mr. Kicklighter taught math for thirty-three years. As a brand-new college graduate, my first teaching team was made up of educators who had a lifetime of experience. One had retired in another state, and the other two had more experience than I had years on Earth.

The textbook that went along with our curriculum was challenging, at best. Many of the kids would have never had an opportunity to grasp some of the concepts. I loved science, and even I had difficulty grasping some of the eighth-grade concepts. At that time, Quality Core Curriculum (QCC) objectives were used to evaluate students. We made it our business to find out the QCC objectives that the students needed to know. We used the textbook as a resource rather than the primary source of lessons. I would bring in supplemental material to teach the course for the year.

With that method, I had a hands-on science class, which remains one of the greatest opportunities I've ever had in my teaching career. I taught science not just by reading; rather, the students learned science by doing science. Some kids did not get the general theories, but they were able to learn by practice. I was able to meet the objectives in a way that would stick with the students. With my method, students became interested in science. I noticed that they were always prepared for class. If there were behavior issues or things that disrupted the class, the punishment would be that the whole class would then do textbook work. All they did was textbook work in their other classes. I made coming to my science class a privilege. We played with science. We did science. It is because we played science and did science, those students learned science.

While at Tubman, I also decided I wanted to do some extracurricular activities, so I began to help coach the football team. What an experience! I started out just assisting for free. I didn't expect anything. I just wanted to help out a little bit. Once I started helping out, the head coach asked me to be the assistant coach. Unbeknownst to me, I would receive a $200 supplement for my help with the football team. Back then, my check was $1,369. An extra $200 for a new graduate just entering the teaching profession was amazing.

Coaching football allowed me to get to know a lot of my students on another level. It put me in the middle of the athletic and academic core of the students. I was able to learn more about where the students were coming from and the challenges they had. That additional time with student athletes, band members, and cheerleaders gave me input into the students' lives. I remember those one-on-one conversations as if they happened yesterday. Those were the tender moments of education, the good moments, where students worked hard and all that mattered was that they learned something. It was a learning experience in which I hopefully contributed to changing how those kids looked at science.

My second year as a teacher I remained at Tubman with my same teaching team. It was during that year, that Dr. Welter, the principal, stopped by my class one day on his rounds. Dr. Welter did not play around. He was a very slender, tall, well-dressed man who commanded excellence. I learned a lot from his leadership style. That day, I was organizing the kids in the hall and moving them from one class to another. Dr. Welter asked me, "Chris, have you ever thought about going into administration?"

I didn't immediately understand what he meant. He continued, "Have you ever thought about being an administrator or an assistant principal?"

"No," I said because I had honestly never thought about it. I was happy teaching science and coaching football. Dr. Welter laughed, saying, "What a waste," as he walked off.

At the end of that year, Dr. Welter fired me from my position as football coach, without explanation. He said he wanted to take the football team in another direction. We had only lost one game that year, so the only other direction didn't make sense. When he fired me from being the football coach, I retaliated by leaving the entire school system.

It dawned on me after leaving the Richmond County school system that I may have made a mistake. I acted out of emotions and reacted harshly. I enjoyed my job and I enjoyed working with the kids in Augusta. I still have a great appreciation for him. A lot of my leadership style really comes from how Dr. Welter ran Tubman Middle School. In retrospect, I should have used that free time to work with Dr. Welter as my mentor. He saw something in me at that point that I didn't see in myself, and he saw something in me that I wasn't interested in seeing. I had no plans of ever being a principal or administrator. My goals were simply to teach school, coach football, and pastor a church. I wanted to live a simple life serving others.

I moved to Douglas County, Georgia, a small county outside of Atlanta. A man named Curtis Briscoe helped me to land a teaching job there. Briscoe first met my wife, who was a teacher at Glenn Hills Middle School in Augusta, through his sister, my wife's seamstress. One day, he overheard my wife mention she was a teacher. Briscoe explained Douglas County Schools was in desperate need of minority teachers. She told him she would come if I could come as well. Apparently, Douglas County needed more African American males than anything else.

We drove up to Douglas County on a Saturday and had an interview. We did not interview with the principal but rather with the administration at the central office. After our interviews, we were both immediately hired and assigned to our schools.

My wife was assigned to Turner Middle School, and I was assigned to Stewart Middle School. At Stewart, I worked under the leadership of Principal Anthony Howell. While at Stewart, Principal Howell came down to my class and said, "You need to think about going back to school and finishing up a leadership degree to become an assistant principal." In my mind, I thought, *Oh Lord, here we go again.* Luckily, I had already reflected on my unnecessarily emotional move from Richmond County, so at this time I decided to learn from my mistakes.

At Stewart, although I was helping with the football team. I wasn't a coach, so I had no excuse to avoid continuing my education. Back at Tubman, I told Dr. Welter that football was the reason I didn't have time to go back to school. I'll never know if that was why he fired me from the team. Either way, I no longer had that excuse. I began taking summer classes at Cambridge College. When I finished that program, I enrolled in Jacksonville State University's leadership program in order to earn leadership certificate so that I could become an assistant principal.

Principal Howell promised that he would hire me as an administrator when I finished getting my certificate. Briscoe also promised that he would look out for me when I finished my degree. Well, in the process of me finishing my degree, Briscoe was released from Douglas County for some impropriety unknown to me. Obviously, he couldn't and didn't fulfill that promise.

Howell was moved from Stewart Middle School to the alternative school. A move to the alternative school was a demotion of sorts. I could not put my finger on why he would have been demoted so quickly and so harshly. I thought he was doing a good job at Stewart Middle School. He was improving the lives of young African American children and making sure that all children learned.

It wasn't until much later that I began to realize that there were racial issues going on in the Douglas County school system. I now believe that race caused Anthony Howell to be reassigned. He may have gone up the wrong tree when he tried to take teachers out of their comfort zone and encouraged pushing the African American kids a little harder.

Because I sacrificed for those certificates, when I finished the credentialing, I wanted to be an assistant principal. On my first assistant principal interview, I didn't get the job because they said I did not pass the leadership test. I don't believe that. The second time I took the test, I went on to the next interview phase.

Douglas County had built a new alternative school out at Chapel Hill. Principal Howell was in charge of the new program, and he was very excited about kids being able to come to school in the day and in the evening. I had one more interview, but I was already excited about joining his team. I would finally get an opportunity to see what it was that Dr. Welter saw in me that I didn't even see in myself.

But when I went on the last interview with him, I never will forget the countenance on his face when I arrived. He looked very sad and very disappointed. When I asked him what was wrong, he said, "They've cut my budget and they've taken the position, so I'm not going to be able to hire you." I tried all I could to laugh it off. I said, "Man, things happen, and they always happen for a reason." I tried to be as courageous as possible and deal with it. But when I got back to the car, I had a breakdown. I was very upset. I didn't understand it. It was then I became more determined to become an assistant principal.

Once I left that office, I began to really look at my credentials. I wanted to be sure I had everything I needed to meet my goal. I re-enrolled in school to work on a specialist degree in leadership. I began to apply for jobs all over the place. Every time a job opened in Douglas County, I applied for it. I applied for every assistant principal's job opening in the Atlanta metro area. Over the next two years, nothing seemed to give. I felt like the new administration at Stewart Middle didn't see the talent in me. I decided that I would move my career over to the DeKalb County school system.

In DeKalb, I was assigned to teach seventh-grade science. I thought moving to a larger county would increase my chances for becoming an administrator. I also felt that Douglas County would only have a limited number of slots for African Americans in administration. While I was there, those slots were filled. I also saw how Anthony Howell was treated and I did not want any part of that.

DeKalb County is the polar opposite of Douglas County. Directly on the other side of the state's capital and largest city. DeKalb was a larger majority African American district. I moved to DeKalb County and I taught in the South DeKalb area. I interviewed with Dr. Emerson in the DeKalb County central office. Dr. Emerson sent me to McNair Middle School just around the corner from my home. A school close to my home was important to me because I didn't want a long commute to work. I wanted to be as close to home as possible.

I walked into the school to meet with the principal and gave him my résumé. He looked at it, nodded his head, and very nonchalantly said, "I'll call you later." I never heard from him.

Afterward, Dr. Emerson called to see if I was still interested in coming to DeKalb County. I told of what happened at McNair. I had worked hard on my credentials and that had been the first time I hadn't at least earned an interview. I knew my résumé spoke well enough to at least get an interview. Dr. Emerson told me not to worry about that. That principal was being moved at the end of the year. In the meantime, she sent me over to interview at Chapel Hill Middle School in Decatur. I was hired on the spot. I taught seventh-grade science at Chapel Hill. I again began to apply for leadership positions at Chapel Hill. Initially, I did not receive any. Then one day in the middle of the year, Assistant Principal Merlin Jones was promoted to principal at Salem Middle School, and his position came open.

Dr. Agnes Flanagan, the principal at Chapel Hill Middle School told me, "I don't know who you know, but whoever you know that's got you over here; you need to call them and tell them that you want that position and then I will hire you." I did, and she immediately pulled me out of the classroom and placed me in the position. At that time, I was moved to the position of administrative assistant, which is like an assistant principal in training. I didn't receive a pay raise, but I did get the opportunity to learn what this assistant principal gig would be all about.

I enjoyed the work, and there was lot of it. I remember after the first day on the job, I went home and said, "I don't think I want to do this." I didn't think that assistant principals worked as hard as they did. I found the work fulfilling, and I did it for the remainder of the year. I worked with the eighth-grade students under the leadership of Dr. Flanagan.

At the end of the year, when it was time to staff for the next year, DeKalb County was crunching numbers and budgets. They were not sure if they were going to hire new assistant principals or reshuffle all of the assistant principals who had already been assigned. I had met the assistant chief of police in Newton County, who I later found out was also on the Board of Education. He became a mentor of mine and still is. At the time, I was pastoring a church in Covington, Georgia, called Almond Turner. I asked him if they were looking for any administrators in Covington. I thought it would be a unique opportunity to work and pastor in the same community. I would have even considered moving there to start having children with my wife.

One of the Covington schools had an opening. I applied with Sandra Smith, the assistant superintendent of human resources for the Covington schools. I interviewed with Dick DuBois at Cousins Middle School. It was a panel interview. After the end of the interview, I went back to the church for Bible study. One of my members worked in the Covington school system. I told them it was an excellent opportunity, but I would never work at Cousins Middle School.

Later, Newton County offered me the job as assistant principal before DeKalb County. I really prayed over whether to extend my commute because I had not moved and I was concerned with driving more than fifty minutes to and from work. I had two choices: drive further or wait longer for DeKalb County to promote me. I prayed. I prayed. I prayed. My mother told me, "A bird in your hand is better than a thousand birds over your head." I accepted the job as assistant principal at Newton County.

One month after accepting the Newton County position, DeKalb County called me in and offered me an assistant principal position in DeKalb County. DeKalb was insistent, almost forceful. I explained that I had taken a job in Newton County, and they told me it didn't matter. They even went so far as to say they had not released me from my contract in DeKalb, so I could not take a job in Newton County.

I called Newton County to tell Sandra Smith that DeKalb County had not released me from my contract. Smith informed me that since I had been promoted, I was automatically released from my contract. Without the contract as a good excuse, I had my reputation on the line. I had accepted the job in Newton County and was a pastor in the community. My word was on the line and felt I couldn't go back. Newton paid less than DeKalb County, but I took the job in Newton County as an assistant principal at Cousins Middle School.

My first year at Cousins, I worked under Dick DuBois. At the end of the year, Dick DuBois retired and I worked under the leadership of Dr. Robert "Bob" Daria. He was the previous assistant principal at Cousins Middle School before being promoted and moving over to Eastside Middle as an assistant principal. Dr. Daria bounced between Cousins, Eastside, and then later became assistant superintendent. He was very instrumental and very helpful. We became personal friends. Dr. Daria died in 2012 as assistant superintendent in Walton County.

At Cousins Middle School, I learned a lot about being an assistant principal. People always talk about it being different in the rural areas than it is in the urban and suburban areas. The reality is that there are challenges in every school district. The children face major issues in every school district. For example, weapons. While in Covington, I took a loaded gun from one student who wanted to help his friend by lying down and hiding the gun under his head. I already mention my first encounter with a gun in Augusta. Like the others, I had to take guns and knives in Atlanta Public Schools. The issues were issues.

After working in Covington and making that long commute, my wife decided she did not want to move to Covington. I also stopped pastoring in Covington, and the commute took a toll on me and my family. At the time, my daughter was only a baby, and I wanted to work closer to home. Now, I had a reason to work closer to home and my career took a back seat to my family, or so I thought. While I was praying over my next steps, there was a news flash that came across about something that had happened at Parks Middle School. The Lord spoke to my spirit I told me to apply for that job. I did.

When I applied for the job, I was called in for an interview. I remember when Tonya Banks and Monique Ross first called me. They told me, "Your application is not complete, and we're pulling applicants to interview." I said to them, "Go ahead and pull some other applicants. I'm going to just be a principal here in Newton County next year." The superintendent in Newton already told me that he had seen my work, and he was going to promote me to principal at one of his schools at the end of the year.

Ross and Banks told me they really wanted me to apply. I went ahead and sent them the complete information that they requested, and sure enough, I was called in for the first interview. The first interview was a panel interview at the SRT level with Michael Pitts and the other teacher leaders. They were sitting around the table interviewing me together. The second interview was at the school. I didn't expect a second interview and certainly not a third. The third interview was with Dr. Hall and Dr. Augustine.

During the third interview, Dr. Augustine asked, "What is my principal going to say in one sentence about me when she calls to check my reference?" I said to her, "He'll tell you that I make his job easy." Sure enough, when she called to check my reference, the first thing Dr. Daria said to her was he makes my job easy. Dr. Augustine started laughing. It was true. I prided myself on making sure that my principal didn't have to do a lot of things. I did all of the things that I could do within my reach so that he could focus on other things that would help to move the school. We worked hand in hand like a team, so I was offered the job.

When I took the job in Atlanta, I had to go meet with Dr. Wendell Clamp, the superintendent in Newton County. I informed him that I had been offered a job in the Atlanta Public Schools and he told me immediately, "You don't want to go work there." I didn't understand it then, but I really understand it now. Dr. Clamp told me, "I've got three schools coming open next year. I promise you, I will put you in one of them. You don't want to go work there." I didn't know how to take his comment that I didn't want to go work there because I knew from the outside that Atlanta Public Schools was an all-black school district. The first thing that came to my mind was there was an element of racism in his comment.

When I reflected on our interactions over time, I began to reflect on the strong relationships that Dr. Clamp had with other people. I couldn't believe it was racism. After the scandal, I could see Dr. Clamp was right.

Even though I ran the course in the Atlanta Public Schools, I had to go through Atlanta to get to where God is going to take me. I now think I understand why Dr. Clamp said I should not work there. I spent six years working for APS, and most of those years were the hardest years of my life.

It is important for anyone interested in what happened in the APS cheating scandal to understand how the socioeconomic makeup and racial makeup of the school system effected how that district operated and how students were able to learn. Each of the different school systems in which I worked had a different flow and culture. They all had their issues and they all had their success. But environmental forces in addition to the educators were the impetus of this scandal.

The Augusta school district was two-thirds African American. Most of the kids lived in housing projects. The focus in Augusta was not on testing. It was on performance. The test was simply a part of the school year. Of course, that was before Annual Yearly Progress was a mandate. The kids took the test, they received their results, and that was it. It had no significant bearing on the teachers or administration. You taught the kids the lessons in the plan. You prepared them for the test with strategies: get plenty of rest; if you don't know a question, skip it; etc. The school kept a record of who passed and who failed when students took the test. But more importantly, Dr. Welter believed in instruction. He believed in teachers teaching. He took no excuses for anything other than that. If you were going to work in that school, you had to teach. However, strategically, Richmond County had no focus. You just taught the kids. He made sure that teachers were teaching and students were learning something.

In Douglas County, it was pretty much the same way. Again, these are pre-AYP and No Child Left Behind days. Anthony Howell was persistent that you were going to teach. He did teacher observations and often did walk-throughs. He wanted to make sure teachers were not sitting behind the desk but rather getting into teaching. As computers in classrooms became more popular, teachers began pulling away and spending time on them. Powell was very clear that you were not going to be behind the computer, but you would be up teaching. Teaching was the focus, not scores, not the test, nor any other specific guidelines.

Cathy Newell, who became the principal once Anthony Howell was demoted, was very involved in the academics. She was not as involved as Principal Howell because she was an office principal, rather than a classroom principal. She did a lot of the paperwork herself. On the other hand, Howell was an in-your-face kind of principal, and you saw him around. He wanted to be a part of classes and personally see the instruction.

District-wide, Douglas County had the demographics of 70/30 Caucasian Americans to African Americans. However, the school in which I worked, Stewart Middle School, was about 95 percent black. The other 5 percent was a mix of white, Latino, and Asian students. Their focused was also on just teaching the kids. There was an emphasis on making sure the kids could pass a test but there was no real focus and pressure on testing.

In DeKalb County, we just did all we could to keep the kids from fighting and to keep the kids in class. The biggest problems were getting kids out of the hall and to stop cutting class. I don't know what our focus was in DeKalb County. We worked hard. We met often. We planned our lessons and we did our best instruction. I never recall an emphasis on testing. We focused on keeping kids safe, keeping them away from harm, keeping them in class, teaching from bell to bell. There were always teachers observing teachers and administrators observing teachers.

It wasn't until Covington that I began to hear about AYP. When I became an assistant principal, testing was one of the things I began to learn. In DeKalb, there was a hired consultant paid with Title I funds to help us to navigate the waters of this new AYP and No Child Left Behind initiatives, which was passed in 2001. I was a new administrator, and AYP was new to everyone.

When I was a new principal, a mother asked, "What percent do you think is an acceptable passage rate for the CRCT?" I remember my first answer was 70 percent. I thought if you get 70 percent of your kids to pass the test, that's a good number for a school. The mother looked at me and said, "I hope your kids, your personal children, are not in the thirty percent." What she really was saying to me was that my goal should have been that 100 percent pass the test. I felt some kind of way, but I didn't say anything. It seemed unreasonable, especially depending on where you taught, to expect 100 percent. But because I was a new administrator, I just dismissed it and did not speak up. The way I understood No Child Left Behind from then on was that by 2014 100 percent of the students would be meeting or exceeding the standards. That bright idea was created in 2001. The year 2014 has arrived and that is as far from true now as it was when the program was created. It wasn't an attainable goal. It couldn't happen.

But with the mandates in place, and being shamed into belief, I started being a part of that 100 percent goal attainability. While I was at Cousins Middle School, it was the first time I remember being brought in to talk about the No Child Left Behind Act. The discussion centered on student performance and meeting the standards. There was no mention of exceeding the standards. I didn't know what that was. We didn't talk about anything else but making sure the kids pass the test.

In Covington and Douglas, we taught children if there's an answer you don't know, leave it blank and it won't count against you. In my mind, I really felt that was the truth. A student didn't lose points for blank answers. So, some students left the whole test blank and still passed. I didn't think through the implications of leaving it blank back then. Of course, I have a different understanding of what possible implications could occur by leaving blank answers now. If we had taught students in Atlanta to leave questions blank, correcting the answers would have been easier. It was the erasure analysis that proved cheating. Throughout the investigation, reports of anonymous complaints of cheating were found. Those complaints never made it past Dr. Hall. Even if they did, without proof of the changed test, no one would have started pointing fingers. Even with the CTB/McGraw Hill analysis, teachers still pled ignorance to the Blue Ribbon Commission. I would never repeat the things I did in the Atlanta Public Schools again. But I can't help to wonder how things may have turned out had I made that one change in our procedure. What evidence would they have had if all the members of my team were silenced by perks?

While I taught at Cousins Middle School for two years, we made AYP each year that I was there. Our subgroups made AYP; our school made AYP. I never participated in any cheating at Cousins. I never heard of any cheating. I wasn't privy of any knowledge of cheating at Cousins. None whatsoever! However, they made AYP every single year. The kids had been taught to leave blank answers because they wouldn't count against you.

Well, when I got to Atlanta, there was a major focus and emphasis on testing. Everything revolved around testing, testing, testing. Here a test, there a test, everywhere a test, test. And there was a major emphasis on performance. The kids were expected to perform at high levels on the test, not in their course work. It was clear. The No Child Left Behind Act was signed into law in 2002. I began at Parks during the spring semester of 2005. The CRCT given in April 2005 was the third year the schools were attempting to meet these requirements.

I recall working on testing throughout the whole time I was at the Atlanta Public Schools.

Everybody focused on testing, and all the results were tied into testing. This was a major culture shift to me. Not only did the administration care about the scores, but they focused on the students not meeting the standards but "exceeding" the standards. I didn't learn that the kids could exceed on the tests until APS.

A school that exceeded on the test got a higher number of tests with correct answers than the average. I had been an assistant principal while the No Child Left Behind Act was being implemented but never heard the term *exceed*. Even when working with the Title I consultant, the issue of "exceeding" was never brought up. I had never had to deal with that prior to coming to the Atlanta Public Schools and didn't know anything about it until teaching in APS.

In addition to focusing on nationally required scores and testing, APS had created this notion of "targets." Meeting targets was much more rigorous than meeting AYP scores. I couldn't imagine then how one could meet the lofty AYP goal of having every child in every school passing the state test by 2014. I certainly didn't think the targets were attainable. They were more unrealistic than AYP.

It was clear that you were making targets in the Atlanta Public Schools. No excuses, no questions. If you didn't make targets, you lost your job. They made examples out of people. So along with all the other social, political, and educational issues that went along with working in the Atlanta Public Schools, administrators felt a pressure and stress around kids passing the test. It didn't matter how well you taught and it didn't matter how much the kids learned. If they did not pass the test, it would have major implications for your school, your staff, and your school leadership.

Chapter 11

The Culture of Teaching and Cheating

I want to go on record as saying all school systems, all communities, have their own cultures and their own set of problems. I never worked in a perfect situation. I always elected to work in the lower-performing schools, because I felt that's where my drive and my passion were. I felt I could meet the needs of more children in the lower-performing and lower socioeconomic schools. There were more children there who needed to see a positive African American male figure and who could relate to someone who had walked in their shoes. I intentionally sought those opportunities out.

I need to be clear, though, that Atlanta Public Schools was a school district that was totally different from the ones in which I had previously worked. In Atlanta, sometimes we were treated like family and other times we were treated like strangers. I didn't get that flip-floppy love-hate relationship in my other schools.

From leadership, there would be times that Dr. Hall and her team would make themselves available to talk, listen, and help you out. Other times they would not, and you were left to figure things out on your own. What I did notice in the latter part of Dr. Hall's tenure, everyone on her team became much friendlier. I don't know if that was just with me, or maybe it was my perception as their poster child, but they seemed more approachable in the later years.

There was no surprise that there were times when they would walk by me in a meeting and not speak. Even if I had said hello, they would not speak. Maybe because I am a southern guy and Dr. Hall and her team came from up north, but that struck me as odd. But if I or any of my contemporaries did something wrong, we were persecuted in front of everybody. Everybody knew about it. It was gangster-like. Everyone knew who got voted off the island. We knew when someone was fired and we always knew why. Imagine walking in a meeting where your leadership team ignores your greeting. You always had a feeling you were next on the chopping block. I am a big man and I have an ego to match. I didn't like to be embarrassed by being ignored, but I refused to be embarrassed by being called out or worse, fired in front of everyone.

New testing regulations and a less than warm and confusing leadership team were not the only problems at APS. I dealt with so many situations in APS that I didn't read about in the textbooks or in the leadership manuals. There were so many situations that were just difficult to deal with. For the protection of my students, I won't reveal any names. There was one situation where a mother had sold her three girls to a man on the bus in exchange for crack. The man took the three girls home. He gave the lady crack and in exchange for "owning" her children. The oldest child was in the sixth grade and was a student in my school. The other two children were elementary school age, and they were at Gideon Elementary School. I never will forget that situation. The "father" had brought the girls to school to register them and everything. Initially, I had been very excited to see this African American single dad being involved in the lives of his children, registering them for school. I had imagined him being one of the involved parents.

I had no clue that something horrible was going on. I had not perceived anything, and there was nothing sticking out to make me think anything out of the ordinary, just a man doing his job as a parent. After the fact, we learned more. Like with many dramatic situations, you added up the clues after the fact.

On one of the days when I had to leave school to go to Bible study, I was preparing to walk out of the building and a young lady came into my office. It was rare; generally, the kids would stop at the secretary's desk and then she would announce them and send them back. This day, the sixth grader said, "I don't want to go home today." I said, "Baby, you have to go home." She said, "No, I don't want to go home today." When she said it the second time, it resonated in my heart. I could literally feel there was more to her not wanting to go home. Initially, I assumed she had gotten in trouble and she didn't know how to tell the parents, so I asked her what happened at school.

I started searching for solutions in my mind before I got the whole story. I was just going to tell the teacher not to speak with the parent just on the phone, but to ask the parent to come to school to explain what had occurred between the child and the parent at home. I felt that the child had a serious fear, so my mind went to the presumption the child could have been being beaten or whipped by the parent. I figured communicating the child's deficiencies to the parent in a different way would help. When I asked the student what happened at school today, she said nothing. Then I asked, "Well, why don't you want to go home?"

I don't know why I asked that question, but when I did, she gave me a story that was the shock of my life. She talked about the fact that her mom had sold her and her sisters on the bus to this man. I asked her how she knew that. She saw the man give her mom the crack, and they had been with him ever since. She told me the man was sexually abusing all of them. As I think about it today, I get angry all over again.

The man would make them sleep in the bed with him. The man and his teenage children would burn the girls with irons, beat them, and do other horrible things. She was able to describe the things with such horrific detail that they had to be true. I fell into my chair in amazement. I was totally dismayed. I sat in my chair for about a minute or more. I was there, but I wasn't. I had gone into a zone like I lost mental consciousness for a moment. I went into an area of unbelief. Things like this don't happen for real. There's no way that this could be happening to this little girl. Protocol was to report first to the SRT director. I wasn't supposed to just call the police immediately. They liked for us to call the SRT and then call the school police before just dialing 911. Nobody from the SRT seemed to care to come. Now I guess because it wasn't related to targets it wasn't important. Afterward, I called 911 and asked for an officer to come to the school. When the officer came to the school, an investigator came out and we sat there and talked. Then the Division of Family and Child Services (DFCS) was called out while we proceeded to make all these calls, the guy I thought was just a "good dad" showed up at the school.

When he walked in, he said, "I'm looking for my daughter. She didn't come home today." By this time, hours had passed. I said, "Well, sir, I've got a major situation going on right now, so I can't help. She's probably out on the football field watching the football team practice." I told him where the football field was. I didn't have time to deal with the "good dad" because I had a situation on my hands. He left, went to the football field, and came back to my office when he didn't find her.

Then I sent him to the gym, saying, "Maybe she's in the gym watching the cheerleaders." He walked to the gym and came back to my office about eight minutes later when he didn't find her. Then I told him I would call transit to see if the bus broke down. Just after I said those words, one of my administrators touched me and said, "That's the man abusing my student." In my mind, I thought, *No. This is not the daddy, this is a good daddy, he's raising his daughters, he brought them to school, no way is it the same guy.* I asked him, "Sir, what's your daughter's name again?" He said the daughter's name. I stepped back into my office and I asked the student her name again. The instant she told me her name, I saw Assistant Principal Reid. I was so glad. As I was about to reach for the man Reid stepped right in front of me and yelled, "You can't do this, Waller. You can't do this. You cannot do this! You cannot do this!"

When I heard that child say her name in the same voice that told me the horrible things this man had done to her and her sisters, I again went to another place in my mind. The man got defensive and started going off. He immediately said, "Well, I don't know what she's been telling y'all." At that point, we had not said anything. He only saw my reaction. He continued, "Whatever she's telling y'all, y'all keep her, I'll put her stuff outside and y'all raise her." He went on and on and on.

That day, we tried to find relatives of the young girl to avoid the children going into the custody of DFCS. I Googled her aunt's name and found out the aunt worked at the hospital about three miles from the school. I called her job and got the aunt on the phone. I told her we had a situation with her nieces and needed her to come to the school. The aunt didn't have a ride, so I said, "Ma'am, I'll come pick you up." I sped to the hospital and back while the police and other administrators stayed with the children. The aunt told me she had been looking for her nieces all over the world. She had been looking everywhere for them, and she was within three miles of them and didn't even know it.

We had to work very hard with the Fulton County DA's office to prosecute the man who had done this. While working with the DA's office, I never realized I would be on the other side of the table in the future. During his case, they found out he was HIV positive when he was molesting the kids. I was called to testify in the case. The guy told me if I testified he'd kill me. But I testified, and he hasn't killed me yet. He was sentenced to something like ninety-nine years. Prior to Parks, I had never dealt with anything on that level. The culture just allowed for that kind of stuff. Some situations were just horrible.

One year, a girl was raped on her way to school and we, the staff, went out and tried to find her rapist. When another young lady was raped going home from school, we called a meeting and tried to get all the community partners together. We organized getting the police out and volunteers out, so we could comb the neighborhood and find her rapist. This had nothing to do with education, tests, or targets, but these were things we dealt with daily. I am listing some of the worse incidents, but there were incidents every single day.

We dealt with parents' and teachers' cars being stolen. Sometimes they were recovered right in the neighborhood. The school was constantly broken into and equipment was stolen. We were constantly completing reports for the police, completing the reports for the school district, and replacing equipment. We later learned one of the parents had all of the equipment at his house. We didn't call the police. We just went down there and asked him for the equipment back. After he wouldn't give it back, we then called the police. The police found out he had all the equipment from every break-in from the last year or two from every school in the area. I don't know if he was doing the burglaries himself, or if he had others doing the work and he would just buy the stolen goods. I guess the plan was to sell the items on the street, but there the equipment was, in his home.

The culture of the families and student issues were not the only differences. It's important to note that the culture as an employee and a professional was different as well. I remember sitting in principals' meetings watching principals pass around Xanax and other prescribed medications in APS. I was floored when I saw it. I was new to the district. They were so open about it that they offered me some. I'm a drug phobic. I'm afraid of what the smallest Tylenol would do to me, so I never messed with any drugs. I quickly said no, but as I continued to work in the district, I began to understand why they used drugs. The culture was that toxic. People under pressure were trying to find ways to relieve themselves, which was their coping mechanism. It was real.

When I compare APS with the other school districts, I have to say that the pressure was not as bad in other school districts. There were issues and pressures that existed but not like APS. There wasn't the same kind of feeling in the other districts. The punishments certainly were not the same. The culture of the Atlanta Public Schools was just toxic, hateful, and gangster-like.

Yet despite the culture, the contention that we worked for these kids doesn't change at any point in this story. I still stand by the fact that had we had an opportunity to focus on the changes in education that were made under my leadership, that cheating would not have to continue to Parks. We would have stopped at the point that the students were achieving on their own. At least that was the plan. Believing that was as naive as the standards of AYP and APS targets. But the investigations came before that opportunity to prove our efforts were right.

After working in multiple school systems, I believe the things we attempted to do at Parks are still the guideline for change. What everyone has to remember is that change is gradual and a slow process that took more time than we were given. If other schools were to examine what changes we implemented, they would see how multifaceted the changes were. We started with making sincere relationships with the neighborhood associations and making business partnerships with large corporations near the school. The red-carpet list of community partners included the Salvation Army, United Way, Georgia State University, the Minister's Alliance, Communities in Schools, Hands on Atlanta, and After School All Stars. We worked with large foundations like Casey Foundation and the Arthur M. Blank Family Foundation to seek both in-kind and financial support for the school and helped provide need services to the families. Their support helped create attendance programs, GED and literacy classes for adults, provide food and learning materials, and start an after-school program for additional tutoring for the kids on the cuff of passing. These groups supplied food, clothing, and computers for students who needed them. Through Parks's partnerships, gained in part by the rising scores, we are able to provide wraparound services such as counseling, working with at-risk students, dental check-ups, and eye exams.

The school, through its partnerships, was able to cut the number of absences in almost half. We implemented ways for students to receive tutoring and to make up assignments, so they were not so far behind. It was even easier for students to catch up because we implemented "Differentiating Instruction," which focuses the teaching based on the individual student's learning type.

We didn't forget that when the staff and students had pride they would work harder. We implemented getting blazers for the students in our school colors, which they wore proudly. For the teachers, we provided planners and notebooks with the school symbol, which our new partners paid for. We changed the physical appearance of the school. We wanted the students to feel safe in their school. I added paintings and murals with the school colors and mascot. Flowers, plants, benches, parking lot maintenance, and other esthetic changes gave the old school a facelift. Teachers were told to put up the work of the students who were doing well up for all to see. Adding an assistant principal to assist with the discipline gave me the time to make all of these things happen.

None of these actions were silver bullets, but they helped to make progress. Starting from behind the eight ball from the elementary school for some of the students compounded the issues but did not stop our attempt.

I recognize in writing this book, no matter how many details I give about the work that was done, people will reflect primarily on the cheating. But there are educators out there who understand the difficulty that causes teachers, according the GOSA investigation to:

- *Erase incorrect answers after the test to change them to the correct answers.*
- *Using clear transparencies to make changing answers easy.*
- *Changing answers together at weekend gatherings and at teachers' personal homes.*
- *Arranging seating in classrooms so that lower performing children could easily cheat off of high performers.*
- *Assigning low performing students to classrooms where the teachers were known to cheat.*

- *Using voice inflection while reading the test to younger students to assist in cheating.*
- *Directly pointing out the answers to students while standing out their desk.*
- *Giving out the answers aloud to students.*
- *Giving the students back their test to make changes.*
- *Teaching the test a day in advance after teachers had a chance to review the questions.*

These things happened. They happened all over APS. But out of the 180 days of school, less than 10 were spent cheating the test and doing the things in the list above. The other 170 days, we educated our children, we supported them, and we loved them. Our children were not cheated.

Epilogue

On April 1, 2015, eleven of the twelve teachers who went to trial were found guilty of racketeering charges. Judge Jerry Baxter, who presided over the longest trial in Georgia's history, handed down the original sentences on April 14. For two weeks, the Superior Court judge questioned his sentences against three of the defendants, Sharon Davis-Williams, Tamara Cotman, and Michael Pitts. Then on April 30, hinting at his looming retirement after thirty years on the bench, Judge Baxter announced their sentence reduction from seven years in prison followed by thirteen years on probation to three years in jail with seven years to follow on probation. The remainder of the convicted educators had a range of sentences that were less than the three reduced sentences. Donald Bullock received a six-month sentence which was served on weekends, a fine, five years' probation and 1,500 hours of community service. Dana Evans received a sentence of five years, one year to be served in jail and the remainder on probation with 1,000 hours of community service. Tabeeka Jordan and Angela Williamson received a five-year penalty with two years to be served in jail, a hefty $5,000 fine and 1,500 hours of community service. Diane Buckner-Webb and Theresia Copeland received the same five-year sentence with one year in jail but a lesser fine of $1,000 and 1,000 hours of community service. Pamela Cleveland received no time in jail but instead five years of probation with a curfew that required her to be home for a year from 7:00 p.m. to 7:00 a.m. Most defendants were treated as First Offenders, which will allow them to remove the conviction from their records if their sentence is completed.

When you include the attorney fees, the seven-month trial, the community service, the public humiliation, and inability to get work in their profession, all of the defendants' penalties were life-changing whether they went to jail or not. Fifteen hundred hours of community service is the equivalent to thirty-eight continuous forty-hour work weeks. Even if those convicted worked a full day on Saturday and Sunday every week, it would take them more than three-and-a-half years to complete the community service requirements. The strain after court for some of the defendants, like Cotman, was a higher cost. Cotman lost her home and her husband, her child was diagnosed with schizophrenia, and she is working odd jobs to make ends meet while she lives with relatives. She and many others had a hard time replacing what they lost.

Some argue the penalty was still too steep for erasing answers. Others calculate the loss to the reputation of the City of Atlanta and the children who matriculated during the years of cheating and feel that the sentence was just and appropriate. Although the dust has yet to completely settle, there were far more people who could not pick a side in the cheating scandal. There is an ongoing debate which questions whether criminal charges accompanied by high bonds was the right way to handle the problem. Others blame the culture of testing and unreasonable requirements from Capitol Hill for the entire scandal. At the end of the trial, no one was vindicated. The students, the school system, the parents, the justice system all left still feeling cheated by everyone. The changed answers on the tests didn't cause the feeling. It was the entire ordeal. Rather, despite the investigation and prosecution, there still was no solution to the bigger problem of failing schools, poor communities, over testing students, and culturally biased testing.

Two of the teachers, Cotman and Williamson, appealed their rulings on a technicality. Their sentences were withheld while their appeal went through the process. The appeal claimed the judge did not give the correct instructions to the jury regarding the RICO statute. Cotman's and Williamson's attorneys argued via their briefs to the court that the incorrect jury instruction led to a confused jury, which convicted them when they shouldn't have. The Georgia Court of Appeals rejected their claims with a smackdown of a ruling. The appeals court not only rejected their argument but also gave a very thorough recount of the evidence presented at trial. The ruling went beyond what normally comes from an appeal of this sort. It left nothing to the imagination. Typically, the Supreme Court of Georgia cites an appellate ruling if the appeal is continued. Appellate judges are generally thorough in their explanations to assist as the appellate process continues. However, in this case, the explanation went beyond what was expected. It could have been the high-profile nature of the case, but the reading of the ruling looked more like contempt for the defendants and their audacity to even go to trial in light of the evidence against them. The Supreme Court of Georgia refused to hear their appeal in 2018.

Christopher Waller, however, has continued to live a life that in retrospect improved after the trial. Once teaching was no longer an option he began to invest in business ventures and opportunities, still preaching, serving the community and supporting his family. Chris cites the scandal as a serious milestone in his life but not a stopping point. Chris's children see him more and he can focus on their education to ensure they get what they need no matter what the school does or does not do. Since writing this memoir, he has moved on. Chris is still willing to share his story to avoid future cheating scandals, uplift the teachers who worked hard, and take the stigma away from the children who attended Parks. But he maintains a lack of interest in profiting from the sales of his story as long as it helps undo some of the pain he caused for his part in the scandal.

In 2014, Atlanta appointed a new school superintendent, Dr. Meria Carstarphen, who worked on changing the reputation of the school district. Enrollment dropped at many schools in APS, leading to consolidation of some of the remaining schools. Enrollment had not taken a hit as drastic since the Atlanta "white-flight" of the 1970s. APS blames the opening of charter schools and the closing of public housing for the decline. No mention of the effect of the cheating scandal on school enrollment has been made. Despite that, the district pushed a program to allow those students affected by the scandal to obtain tutoring and educational assistance into 2021. There are approximately eight hundred students graduating high school in 2019 as the last class that was enrolled during the scandal.

The Annie-Casey foundation, although still supporting programs in APS, has removed all traces of the "Beating the Odds" article and instead has a similar publication about their investment into the Atlanta Public School system called "Changing the Odds." The updated publication no longer focuses on testing and school environment but rather on the community, school, and family economic impacts on education.

What did not change was the need for private investment into Atlanta Public Schools. The public sector still provided resources and funds to the school system well into 2018. Although not as healthy as the $147 million in investments received in 2013 before the scandal reached full bloom, the investments continued because a booming city like Atlanta must have a strong education system. As any investor knows, investing during a down market increases the chances of growth and profit. The APS school superintendent Dr. Carstarphen asked two years to the date of the conclusion of the trial, "Does the community have the will to invest in its public schools?" That answer remains to be seen.

What is known is that the culture of Atlanta Public Schools did not change completely under the watchful eye of the entire world.

After the trial and conviction there were massive replacements of administrators. Yet even new administrators were caught cheating, having sex on campus with parents, and even fighting in the schools. Maybe you can remove the teachers from the scandal but cannot remove the scandal from an entire system.

In March 2019, a major cheating scandal at the university level was announced. The Hollywood elite and other financially successful individuals were caught paying to get their children into top schools. From paying proctors to take test for the children, paying to get disability modifications during testing, or paying for a position on an athletic team, parents paid millions of dollars cheating their children into school. This case, unlike APS, was investigated and broken by the Federal Bureau of Investigation rather than a local newspaper. Like APS, the accused received high bonds and are facing jail time unless they confess early.

It is clear it is time we look at the American education system from free pre-K, to public education, to testing, to education beyond grade school, to the high cost of a college education and student loan debt. Since the APS scandal, no one has had a serious discussion. It is our hope this book will help to change that.

—LaDawn B. Jones

Sentences and Bonds of the APS Scandal

Ingrid Abella-Sly
- Former teacher at Humphries Elementary.
- $50,000.00 bond.
- Pleaded guilty on Dec. 13, 2013, to a misdemeanor obstruction charge and admitted she gave students answers on standardized tests.
- Sentenced to probation.

Wendy Ahmed
- Former teacher at Humphries Elementary.
- $50,000.00 bond.
- Pleaded guilty Dec. 19, 2013, to a misdemeanor count of obstruction for telling her students the correct answers.
- Sentenced to Probation.

Derrick Broadwater
- Former teacher at Dobbs Elementary.
- $50,000.00 bond.
- Pleaded guilty on Jan. 6, 2014, to one misdemeanor count of obstruction.
- Sentenced to probation.

Lucious Brown
- Former principal of Kennedy Middle.
- $100,000.00 bond.
- Pleaded guilty on Jan. 17, 2014, to interfering with government property for erasing and changing students' answers.
- Sentenced to probation.

Diane Buckner-Webb

- Former teacher at Dunbar Elementary.
- $50,000.00 bond.
- Tried for Racketeering, false statements and writings
- Found GUILTY of violation of Racketeer Influenced and Corrupt Organizations Act. GUILTY of two counts of False Statements and Writings.
- Sentenced to one year in prison, four years probation, 1,000 hours of community service and a $1,000 fine. Given first-offender status.

Donald Bullock

- Former testing coordinator at BE Usher/ Collier Heights Elementary.
- $1 million bond.
- Tried for Racketeering, false statements or writings, false swearing
- Found GUILTY of violation of RICO Act. NOT GUILTY of one count of False Statements and Writings. GUILTY of two counts of False Statements and Writings. GUILTY of False Swearing.
- Pleaded after trial and before sentencing.
- Sentenced to 6 months of weekends in jail, 5 years of probation, 1,500 hours of community service, a $5,000.00 fine and an apology. Given first-offender status.

Pamela Cleveland

- Former teacher at Dunbar Elementary.
- $50,000.00 bond.
- Tried for Racketeering, false statements and writings
- Found GUILTY of violation of Racketeer Influenced and Corrupt Organizations Act. GUILTY of two counts of False Statements and Writings.
- Sentenced after taking a plea deal on the day of sentencing.

- Sentenced to five years of probation with one year of home confinement, 1,000 hours of community service and a $1,000 fine. Given first-offender status.

Theresia Copeland
- Former testing coordinator at Benteen Elementary.
- $1 million bond reduced to a $50,000.00 bond.
- Tried for Racketeering, false statements or writings, theft by taking
- Found GUILTY of violation of Racketeer Influenced and Corrupt Organizations Act. NOT GUILTY of Theft by Taking. GUILTY of one count of False Statements and Writings. One count of False Statements and Writings DISMISSED.
- Sentenced to one year in prison, four years probation, 1,000 hours of community service and a $1,000 fine. Given first-offender status.

Tamera Cotman
- Former School Reform Team executive director.
- Tried for Racketeering and influencing witnesses; found not guilty of trying to influence a witness
- Found GUILTY of violation of Racketeer Influenced and Corrupt Organizations Act
- Sentenced to three years in prison, seven years probation, 2,000 hours of community service and a $25,000 fine.

Dessa Curb
- Former teacher at Dobbs Elementary.
- $60,000.00 bond.
- Tried for Racketeering, false statements and writings
- Found NOT GUILTY of violation of Racketeer Influenced and Corrupt Organizations Act. NOT GUILTY of two counts of False Statements and Writings.

Willie Davenport
- Former principal at D.H. Stanton Elementary.
- $100,000.00 bond.
- Passed away in September 2013 while still scheduled to go on trial.

Clarietta Davis
- Former principal of Venetian Hills Elementary.
- $100,000.00 bond.
- Pleaded guilty on Jan. 6, 2014, to felony false statements due to changing answers from wrong to right on standardized tests in 2007 and 2008.
- Sentenced to probation.

Sharon Davis-Williams
- Former School Reform Team executive director.
- $25,000.00 bond.
- Tried for Racketeering, false swearing, false statements and writing
- Found GUILTY of violation of RICO Act. NOT GUILTY of two counts of False Statements and Writings. Earlier charge of False Swearing dismissed.
- Sentenced to three years in prison, seven years probation, 2,000 hours of community service and a $25,000 fine.

Carol Dennis
- Secretary at Kennedy Middle.
- $20,000.00 bond.
- Pleaded guilty on Jan. 6, 2014, to misdemeanor obstruction for correcting student answers.
- Sentenced to probation.

Dana Evans
- Former principal of Dobbs Elementary.
- $100,000.00 bond.
- Tried for Racketeering, false statements and writings
- Found GUILTY of violation of Racketeer Influenced and Corrupt Organizations Act. NOT GUILTY of three counts of False Statements and Writings. GUILTY of one count of False Statements and Writings.
- Sentenced to one year in prison, four years probation and 1,000 hours of community service. Given first-offender status.

Sheila Evans
- Former teacher at Benteen Elementary.
- $50,000.00 bond.
- Pleaded guilty on Dec. 16, 2013, to misdemeanor obstruction.
- Sentenced to probation.

Millicent Few
- Former APS human resources director.
- $10,000.00 bond.
- Pleaded guilty on Feb. 17, 2014, to misdemeanor malfeasance for assisting staff to shred a critical internal investigation report.
- Sentenced to Probation.

Tameka Goodson
- Former instructional coach at Kennedy Middle.
- $40,000.00 bond.
- Pleaded guilty on Dec. 20, 2013, to obstruction and for changing answers on student standardized tests.
- Sentenced to probation.

Beverly Hall

- Former superintendent of Atlanta Public Schools.
- $7.5 million bond cash bond reduced to $200,000.00 bond.
- Died of breast cancer on March 2, 2015.
- Charged with Violation of Racketeer Influenced and Corrupt Organizations Act, False Statements and Writings, Theft by Taking, and False Swearing

Gloria Ivey

- Former teacher at Dunbar Elementary.
- $50,000.00 bond.
- Pleaded guilty on Jan. 6, 2014, to one misdemeanor obstruction for admonishing students for not correcting answers and pointing out the correct answers in some cases.
- Sentenced to probation.

Tabeeka Jordan

- Former assistant principal of Deerwood Academy.
- $10,000.00 bond.
- Tried for Racketeering, false statements and theft by taking
- Found GUILTY of violation of Racketeer Influenced and Corrupt Organizations Act. NOT GUILTY of False Statements and Writings. NOT GUILTY of Theft by Taking.
- Sentenced to two years in prison, three years probation, 1,500 hours of community service and a $5,000 fine. Given first-offender status.

Francis Mack

- Former testing coordinator at D.H. Stanton Elementary.
- $50,000.00 bond.
- Pleaded guilty on Dec. 20, 2013, to obstruction for not disclosing previous information about cheating to investigators.
- Sentenced to probation.

Lera Middlebrooks
- Former testing coordinator at Dunbar Elementary.
- Pleaded guilty on Dec. 18, 2013, to misdemeanor obstruction for giving teachers answer sheets for standardized tests.
- Sentenced to probation.

Starlette Mitchell
- Former teacher at Parks Middle.
- $50,000.00 bond.
- Pleaded guilty on Jan. 6, 2014, to misdemeanor obstruction.
- Sentenced to probation.

Kimberly Oden
- Former teacher at Parks Middle.
- $50,000.00 bond.
- Pleaded guilty on Jan. 6, 2014, to one misdemeanor count of obstruction.
- Sentenced to probation.

Michael Pitts
- Former School Reform Team executive director.
- $25,000.00 bond.
- Tried for Racketeering and influencing witnesses
- Found GUILTY of violation of Racketeer Influenced and Corrupt Organizations Act. GUILTY of Influencing Witnesses.
- Sentenced to three years in prison, seven years probation, 2,000 hours of community service and a $25,000 fine. Three years to serve concurrent on Influencing Witnesses conviction.

Gregory Reid
- Former assistant principal of Parks Middle.
- $50,000.00 bond.

- Pleaded guilty on Dec. 16, 2013, to two counts of obstruction.
- Sentenced to probation.

Shani Robinson
- Former teacher at Dunbar Elementary.
- $40,000.00 bond.
- Tried for Racketeering, false statements and writings
- Found GUILTY of violation of Racketeer Influenced and Corrupt Organizations Act. GUILTY of False Statements and Writings.
- Sentenced to one year in prison, four years probation, 1,000 hours of community service and a fine of $1,000.

Sheridan Rogers
- Former testing coordinator at Gideons Elementary.
- $50,000.00 bond.
- Pleaded guilty on Dec. 20, 2013, to obstruction for giving teachers access to their tests and answer sheets.
- Sentenced to Probation.

Armstead Salters
- Former principal of Gideons Elementary.
- $100,000.00 bond.
- Pleaded guilty on Dec. 19, 2013, to a felony making false statements and writings since he signed off on tests taken by his students.
- Sentenced to probation.

Shayla Smith
- Former teacher at Dobbs Elementary.
- $60,000.00 bond.
- Pleaded guilty on Dec. 17, 2013, to a single misdemeanor count of obstruction for changing students' answers in 2007.

- Sentenced to probation.

Lisa Terry
- Former teacher at Humphries Elementary.
- $50,000.00 bond.
- Pleaded guilty on Nov. 20, 2013, to a misdemeanor charge of obstruction for allowing students to change their answers. She was the first to enter a guilty plea.
- Sentenced to probation.

Christopher Waller
- Former principal of Parks Middle.
- $100,000.00 bond.
- Pleaded guilty on Feb. 21, 2014, to a felony count of making false statements.
- Sentenced to probation.

Sandra Ward
- Former testing coordinator at Parks Middle.
- $50,000.00 bond.
- Pleaded guilty on Feb. 21, 2014, to misdemeanor obstruction for correcting answers on student's test.
- Sentenced to probation.

Angela Williamson
- Former teacher at Dobbs Elementary.
- Tried for Racketeering, false statements and writings, false swearing
- Found GUILTY of violation of Racketeer Influenced and Corrupt Organizations Act. GUILTY of four counts of False Statements and Writings.
- Sentenced to two years in prison, three years probation, 1,500 hours of community service and a $5,000 fine. Given first-offender status.

Discussion Questions

1. Were the students cheated? If so, by whom? The teachers, the administration, or the No Child Left Behind Act requirements?

2. What is the take on the author's acceptance of responsibility? Does it matter that it took so long? Does his version of the facts appear to be an explanation or an excuse?

3. Does this scandal prove that standardized testing is not a fair way to measure a student's or teacher's success?

4. Do you agree with the criminal prosecution and the method of prosecution? Does the fact that teachers received bonus money make the actions more criminal?

5. Was cheating one portion of a larger negative culture of drugs, sex, and violence or was cheating the cause of the culture that included sex, drugs, and violence within the school system?

6. What effect did the urban location, socio-economic status, or race of the community have on the start of the scandal?

Acronyms and Abbreviations

ADA   Assistant District Attorney

AEF   Atlanta Education Fund

AJC   Atlanta Journal–Constitution

APS   Atlanta Public Schools

AYP   Adequate Yearly Progress

BRC   Blue Ribbon Commission

CME   Christian Methodist Episcopal

CRCT   Criterion-Referenced Competency Tests

DA   District Attorney

GBI   Georgia Bureau of Investigation

GOSA   Governor's Office for Student Achievement

QCC   Quality Core Curriculum

WTR   wrong-to-right

Cheating but Not Cheated

www.ingramcontent.com/pod-product-compliance
Lightning Source LLC
Chambersburg PA
CBHW060832050426
42453CB00008B/666